Here is the sequel to the critically-acclaimed *A NEW APPROACH TO PLAY AND DEFENSE,* in which Eddie Kantar introduced a concept new to bridge problem books. In that book, as in this, fifty brand-new hands are laid out, and the bidding reviewed. Then you, as declarer, must plan the play of the hand to make the contract.

The same fifty hands (or, sometimes, very similar hands altered just enough to give you a fighting chance) are then presented again, seen from the vantage point of the defense. This time, you must figure out how to defeat the contract!

All the solutions are given, together with Eddie Kantar's humorous analysis of problems, bridge and bridge players. A brief appendix of themes allows you to review individual problems addressing particular situations.

This book may be more fun than actually playing bridge! Certainly, it helps make your play more fun — and better.

BRIDGE BOOKS BY EDWIN B. KANTAR

Introduction to Declarer's Play
Introduction to Defender's Play
> *– Prentice-Hall*

Defend with Your Life
> *– Faber & Faber*

Gamesman Bridge
> *– Liveright Publishers*

Bridge Bidding Made Easy
Defensive Play Complete
Improve Your Bidding Skills
Test Your Play, Vol. I
Test Your Play, Vol. II
Kantar for the Defense, Vol. I
Kantar for the Defense, Vol. II
Bridge Humor
> *– Wilshire Book Co.*

The Kantar on Bridge Series:
   A New Approach to Play and Defense
   A New Approach to Play and Defense, Vol. 2

> *– HDL Publishing Co.*

A NEW APPROACH TO
PLAY AND DEFENSE
VOLUME 2

Edwin B. Kantar

HDL PUBLISHING COMPANY

HDL PUBLISHING COMPANY,

A Division Of

HDL COMMUNICATIONS, INC.
702 RANDOLPH AVENUE
COSTA MESA, CA 92626, USA

10 9 8 7 6 5 4 3 2 1

PRINTED IN THE UNITED STATES OF AMERICA

ISBN 0-937359-22-X

INTRODUCTION

Due to the overwhelmingly enthusiastic response (three letters) to my last book *"A New Approach to Play and Defense"*, I have decided to write a sequel. The imaginative title to my new book is *"A New Approach to Play and Defense, Vol. II."* Would anybody like to guess what the title of the third book in the series will be?

With the help of friends who have supplied several "two way" hands, I have gathered together 102 (the front and back covers count, you know) play and defense problems.

Those of you who waded through the last book know that each problem has a mate. For example, the first 25 problems in the book are play problems. The second 25 are the matching defensive problems.

Let's say that you are to play 4 ♠ on problem 8 in the Play section. If you do everything right you will make the hand. Later, when you come to problem 8 in the defensive section, you will be defending 4 ♠. Because I have switched a card or two you will be able to defeat 4 ♠. So what's the point?

The point is simply this: if you remember what you did to make 4 ♠, you might be able to work out what you must do to defeat 4 ♠. Play and defense are not that dissimilar.

Section III is comprised of 25 defensive problems and Section IV 25 play problems. Again the problems are matched. What you have to do to defeat a contract will eventually help you make that same contract when you play it later.

Most of the bidding will follow standard lines. I am assuming a 15-17 point notrump range unless otherwise stipulated. Weak Twos and Weak Jump Overcalls are also the norm.

Many of the problems have more than one question. In order for you to get the most out of the problems, you should glance to the immediate right of the title of the problem. If you see something like: (1) (2) that means the answers to questions one and two will be found beneath the questions. Therefore, try your best to avoid reading beneath those questions until you have decided what to do.

The back of the book has an appendix which lists the theme(s) of the problems. This should help you in case you actually miss a problem or two. You can check the themes and see where you need work.

I think the problems in this book are slightly harder than those in the previous one. I can only hope the one liners are not too corny.

Finally, I would really be remiss not to thank my ever-growing staff of proofreaders. This time the list includes Lucy Gellner, Jennifer Evans, Steve Cohen, Ed Davis, and above all, Ann Faget, who can find things that are unfindable. Enjoy.

Edwin B. Kantar
Los Angeles

CONTENTS

SECTION I (PLAY HANDS)

SECTION II (DEFENSIVE HANDS)

SECTION III (DEFENSIVE HANDS)

SECTION IV (PLAY HANDS)

Section I
PLAY

(1) UNSTOPPED SUIT

Neither side vulnerable
Dealer South

North
♠ A 7 5
♡ 7 2
♢ A K Q 6
♣ J 9 4 2

South
♠ K J 4
♡ J 10 3
♢ J 9 7
♣ K Q 8 3

South	West	North	East
Pass	Pass	1 ♢	Pass
2 NT	Pass	3 NT	All Pass

Opening Lead: ♠ 10 (Zero or two
higher honors)

What do you think is your best chance to steal this game?

UNSTOPPED SUIT (SOLUTION)

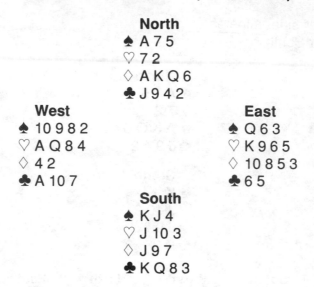

North
♠ A 7 5
♡ 7 2
◇ A K Q 6
♣ J 9 4 2

West
♠ 10 9 8 2
♡ A Q 8 4
◇ 4 2
♣ A 10 7

East
♠ Q 6 3
♡ K 9 6 5
◇ 10 8 5 3
♣ 6 5

South
♠ K J 4
♡ J 10 3
◇ J 9 7
♣ K Q 8 3

Win the first spade in <u>dummy</u> and lead a low club to the <u>queen</u>. If West has the ♣ A, he will be hard pressed to shift to a heart. By winning in dummy rather than letting the lead ride around to your hand, you have obfuscated the spade position;   by playing the ♣ Q you may give West the impression that East has the ♣ K.

If the ♣ Q holds, you can try leading a low club. If West happens to have the ♣ A and ducks again, you have nine tricks with the queen of spades marked in the East hand.

Notice that you are trying to fool West, not East. East knows the spade position because of the East-West lead convention.

KEY LESSON POINTERS

1. WHEN TRYING TO CONCEAL STRENGTH IN THE SUIT THE OPPONENTS HAVE LED, WINNING IN DUMMY IS USUALLY BEST.
2. WHEN ONE OPPONENT HAS A CLEARER IDEA FROM THE LEAD WHAT IS GOING ON, TRY TO TRAP THE OPPONENT WHO IS MORE IN THE DARK.
3. LEADING LOW TOWARD A KING EARLY IN THE HAND USUALLY SHOWS POSSESSION OF THE QUEEN. LEADING TOWARD A KING-QUEEN COMBINATION AND PLAYING THE QUEEN IS FREQUENTLY MORE DECEPTIVE, PARTICULARLY AGAINST EXPERIENCED OPPONENTS.

(2) WHOSE SUIT IS BETTER?

East-West vulnerable
Dealer South

North
♠ J 8
♡ 6 2
♢ 5 4
♣ A K Q 10 9 8 7

South
♠ Q 10 5 4
♡ A Q
♢ A K Q J 9 8 6
♣ –

South	West	North	East
1 ♢	Pass	2 ♣	Pass
3 ♢	Pass	5 ♣	Pass
5 ♢	All Pass		

Opening Lead: ♡ J

You win the ♡ Q. What is your plan?

WHOSE SUIT IS BETTER? (SOLUTION)

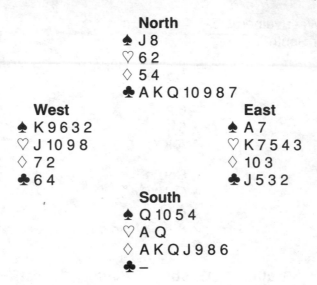

North
♠ J 8
♡ 6 2
◇ 5 4
♣ A K Q 10 9 8 7

West
♠ K 9 6 3 2
♡ J 10 9 8
◇ 7 2
♣ 6 4

East
♠ A 7
♡ K 7 5 4 3
◇ 10 3
♣ J 5 3 2

South
♠ Q 10 5 4
♡ A Q
◇ A K Q J 9 8 6
♣ –

Draw trumps and lead a low spade toward dummy. If West panics and wins the trick, you can lose no more than two spades.

If West plays low, insert the ♠ 8. It is your best chance to lose only two spade tricks- playing West for the ♠ 9.

Leading spades before drawing trumps is even more risky than finessing the ♠ 8. Anytime spades are 5-2 (30%), you leave yourself open to a spade overruff of dummy. Furthermore, if spades are 4-3, the opponents will usually be able to lead two rounds of trumps to frustrate any attempt to ruff a spade in dummy.

KEY LESSON POINTERS

1. AFTER THE OPENER MAKES A JUMP REBID, A JUMP REBID BY THE RESPONDER IN HIS ORIGINAL SUIT IS SUPPOSED TO SHOW A SOLID SUIT.
2. THE BEST PLAY FOR TWO TRICKS WITH J8 OPPOSITE Q10xx IS TO LEAD LOW TO THE EIGHT.

(3) MIRRORS (1)

East-West vulnerable
Dealer South

North
♠ A 3 2
♡ A J 9 8 6
♢ A 6 5
♣ K 4

South
♠ Q J 8
♡ K Q 10 4 3
♢ K 7 4
♣ A J

South	West	North	East
1 NT	Pass	2 ♢*	Pass
3 ♡	Pass	6 ♡	All Pass

*Transfer

Opening Lead:　♢ J

You win the ♢ K and draw trumps in two rounds ending in your hand, East discarding a club.
1.　Which card do you lead at this point? Why?
　　The ♠ J because you do **not** want it covered if West has the ♠ K.
2. Assume the ♠ J holds. How do you continue?
3. Assume West covers the ♠ J. How do you continue?

MIRRORS (SOLUTION)

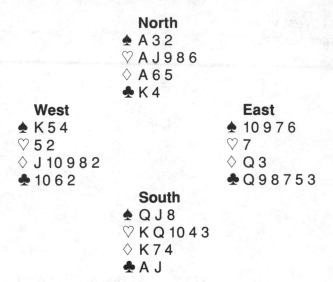

North
♠ A 3 2
♡ A J 9 8 6
♢ A 6 5
♣ K 4

West
♠ K 5 4
♡ 5 2
♢ J 10 9 8 2
♣ 10 6 2

East
♠ 10 9 7 6
♡ 7
♢ Q 3
♣ Q 9 8 7 5 3

South
♠ Q J 8
♡ K Q 10 4 3
♢ K 7 4
♣ A J

2. Your best bet now is to strip the clubs and play ace and a diamond. If West has to win this trick he will be endplayed. He will either have to lead a spade from the king or surrender a ruff and a sluff.

3. Now your best bet is to try to throw East in with a spade after stripping the clubs and playing a second diamond. If East has only two diamonds and has to win the third round of spades, he, too, will have to surrender a ruff and a sluff allowing you to shake that miserable third diamond.

KEY LESSON POINTERS

1. WHEN BOTH HANDS HAVE THE SAME DISTRIBUTION (MIRRORED), YOU MUST BE ON THE LOOKOUT FOR STRIP AND END PLAYS.

2. WHEN LEADING ONE OF SEVERAL EQUAL HONORS, DECIDE BEFOREHAND WHETHER IT IS TO YOUR ADVANTAGE TO HAVE THE HONOR COVERED OR NOT. IF IT IS, LEAD THE HIGHER OR HIGHEST OF EQUAL HONORS; IF NOT, THE LOWER OR LOWEST.

3. WHEN HOLDING Axx OPPOSITE Kxx IN A SUIT CONTRACT THERE ARE CHANCES TO EITHER AVOID A LOSER IN THE SUIT OR TO USE THE LOSER TO YOUR ADVANTAGE.

    (a) YOU CAN CASH THE AK AND PLAY A THIRD ROUND OF THE SUIT. THE PLAYER WHO WINS THE TRICK WILL EITHER HAVE TO BREAK ANOTHER SUIT OR GIVE YOU A RUFF AND A SLUFF.

    (b) CASH THE AK AND THEN THROW IN THE PLAYER WHO DOES NOT HAVE ANY MORE CARDS IN THE Axx OPPOSITE Kxx SUIT. IF THE HAND HAS BEEN ENTIRELY STRIPPED, HE WILL HAVE TO GIVE YOU A RUFF AND A SLUFF.

(4) WATCHING EVERYTHING (1) (2) (3)

Both sides vulnerable
Dealer South

North
- ♠ Q J 10 9 4 2
- ♡ A K 3
- ◇ A 5
- ♣10 6

South
- ♠ A
- ♡ Q J 9 8 7 2
- ◇ Q 3
- ♣ A 9 7 5

South	West	North	East
1 ♡	Pass	1 ♠	Pass
2 ♡	Pass	3 ◇	Pass
3 NT	Pass	4 ♡	Pass
4 NT*	Pass	5 ♣**	Pass
6 ♡	All Pass		

*Roman Key Card Blackwood
**Zero or three key cards

Opening Lead: ◇ J

1. Do you duck this around or do you go up? Why?
   You go up because you want to make the hand! The real reason is that you should be able to work with the spades without risking the diamond play.
2. Which cards do you play to the next two tricks?
   The ♠ A and the ♡ 7 to dummy, all following.
3. Now what?
   Lead the ♠ Q and if not covered, discard the ◇ Q. Let's say you lead the ♠ Q, but East, that scoundrel, ruffs!
4. And now?

WATCHING EVERYTHING (SOLUTION)

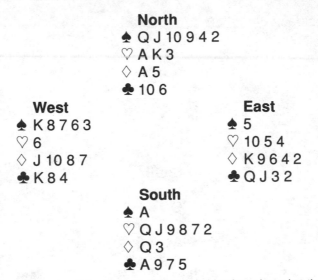

North
- ♠ Q J 10 9 4 2
- ♡ A K 3
- ◇ A 5
- ♣ 10 6

West
- ♠ K 8 7 6 3
- ♡ 6
- ◇ J 10 8 7
- ♣ K 8 4

East
- ♠ 5
- ♡ 10 5 4
- ◇ K 9 6 4 2
- ♣ Q J 3 2

South
- ♠ A
- ♡ Q J 9 8 7 2
- ◇ Q 3
- ♣ A 9 7 5

4.   And now you get to show off. Overruff and lead any heart but the deuce to dummy, drawing trumps, and lead the ♠ J discarding that infernal ◇ Q. No matter what West returns you can win, enter dummy with that carefully preserved ♡ 2 to dummy's ♡ 3, and discard your remaining clubs on dummy's good spades. What a player.

KEY LESSON POINTERS

1. WHENEVER YOU ARE TRYING TO ESTABLISH A LONG SUIT IN DUMMY, BE PARTICULARLY CAREFUL OF YOUR ENTRIES IN THE TRUMP SUIT. SOMETIMES THE TRUMP DEUCE CAN BE THE MOST VALUABLE CARD YOU OWN. FOR EXAMPLE, INTER--CHANGE THE ♡ 2 AND THE ♡ 3 AND SEE IF YOU CAN MAKE THE HAND.

2. AN EASY WAY TO ESTABLISH A LONG SUIT THAT IS MISSING ONE HONOR IS TO MAKE A LOSER ON LOSER PLAY. HERE, FOR EXAMPLE, IF EAST FOLLOWS TO THE SECOND SPADE, DISCARD YOUR ◇ Q, IMMEDIATELY SETTING UP YOUR REMAINING SPADES FOR CLUB DISCARDS ONCE WEST HAS TAKEN HIS KING.

3. WITH A CHOICE OF RUFFING LOSERS IN THE DUMMY (CLUBS) OR ESTABLISHING DUMMY'S LONG SUIT (SPADES) IF ENTRIES PERMIT, GO FOR DUMMY'S LONG SUIT.

(5) MISH MASH (1)

East-West vulnerable
Dealer South

North
♠ A 8 7
♡ K Q 8 3
◇ 8 7
♣ J 10 7 2

South
♠ 2
♡ A J 2
◇ A K 9 4 3 2
♣ A K 8

South	West	North	East
1 ◇	Pass	1 ♡	Pass
3 ♣	Pass	4 ♣	Pass
4 ♡	Pass	4 ♠	Pass
5 NT*	Pass	6 ♣	All Pass

*Pick the best slam

Opening Lead: ♠ 4

I know, I know, you never would be in such a mess. But humor me just this once and try to make 6 ♣.

You win the ♠ A and run the ♣ J which holds. When you lead a second club to your hand, East produces the ♣ Q.
1.   Assuming that trumps are 4-2, how should you proceed? You should duck a diamond.
2.   Assume the opponents win and play a spade forcing you to ruff with your last trump. Now what?

MISH MASH (SOLUTION)

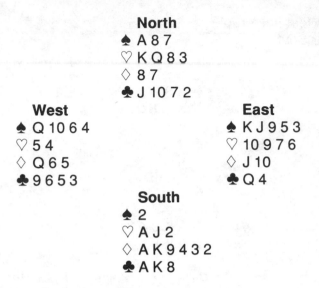

North
♠ A 8 7
♡ K Q 8 3
◇ 8 7
♣ J 10 7 2

West
♠ Q 10 6 4
♡ 5 4
◇ Q 6 5
♣ 9 6 5 3

East
♠ K J 9 5 3
♡ 10 9 7 6
◇ J 10
♣ Q 4

South
♠ 2
♡ A J 2
◇ A K 9 4 3 2
♣ A K 8

2.   Cash <u>one</u> high heart and begin to run diamonds through West.

If West ruffs, overruff, draw the last trump and claim. If West refuses to ruff you can discard dummy's last spade and the remaining three hearts on the diamonds. With the lead in the South hand at trick twelve, dummy takes the last two trump tricks.

All you really need is 3-2 diamonds to bring home the slam once you assume that East is telling the truth with the ♣ Q.

KEY LESSON POINTERS

1. WHEN YOU ARE IN THE WRONG CONTRACT, DO NOT DESPAIR AND DO NOT START PLANNING YOUR POST-MORTEM ARGUMENT. CONCENTRATE ON THE MATTER AT HAND AND FORGET EVERYTHING ELSE. YOUR PARTNER IS SURE TO BRING UP THE ISSUE ONE MICROSECOND AFTER THE HAND IS OVER ANYWAY.

2. WHEN PLANNING A TRUMP COUP YOU MUST ALLOW FOR THE OPPONENT WITH THE MISSING TRUMPS TO DISCARD ON YOUR WINNERS RATHER THAN TRUMP. YOU MUST CONSIDER HOW MANY DISCARDS YOU HAVE ON YOUR LONG SUIT.

    FOR INSTANCE, IN THIS CASE YOU CAN MAKE FOUR DISCARDS FROM DUMMY ON THE DIAMONDS, BUT THERE ARE FIVE CARDS IN THE DUMMY, FOUR HEARTS AND ONE SPADE. SO, CASH ONE HEART BEFORE RUNNING THE DIAMONDS TO PREVENT WEST FROM THROWING AWAY HEARTS ON DIAMONDS AND THEN RUFFING A HEART IN A THREE CARD END POSITION. YOU ARE TRYING FOR A TWO CARD END POSITION, IF WEST REFUSES TO RUFF DIAMONDS.

(6) BOTH SIDES BID NOTRUMP

North-South vulnerable
Dealer East

North
♠ 2
♡ A 8 3
◇ 10 9 4 2
♣ A K J 9 6

South
♠ Q 10 8 7
♡ K 10 5
◇ K J 3
♣ Q 10 7

East	South	West	North
1 NT*	Pass	2 ♠	Dbl.
Pass	3 NT	All Pass	

*13-15

Opening Lead: ♠ 4

East plays the ♠ J. How do you place the missing honors around the table, and what is your plan?

BOTH SIDES BID NOTRUMP (SOLUTION)

North
♠ 2
♡ A 8 3
◇ 10 9 4 2
♣ A K J 9 6

<table>
<tr><td>West</td><td>East</td></tr>
<tr><td>♠ A 9 6 4 3</td><td>♠ K J 5</td></tr>
<tr><td>♡ 9 7 6 2</td><td>♡ Q J 4</td></tr>
<tr><td>◇ 8 6</td><td>◇ A Q 7 5</td></tr>
<tr><td>♣ 5 4</td><td>♣ 8 3 2</td></tr>
</table>

South
♠ Q 10 8 7
♡ K 10 5
◇ K J 3
♣ Q 10 7

For openers, East must have either the ace or king of spades. If West had both of those cards East would have opened 1NT with only 10 high card points.

Once you have concluded that West has a high spade honor, then East must have all of the other missing honors, save, perhaps, the ♡ J.

As long as you can be sure that East has both the ace and queen of diamonds, then the only problem is to avoid the loss of <u>four</u> spade tricks when East gets in with the ◇ A.

Notice that if you take the first spade, that is exactly what will happen. East will win the ◇ A and play the king and a spade. You lose four spades and a diamond. However, if you duck the opening lead, you still retain a spade stopper, and the opponents can only take three spades along with their ◇ A.

KEY LESSON POINTERS

1. ADD YOUR HIGH CARD POINTS TO DUMMY'S HIGH CARD POINTS TO DETERMINE HOW MANY HIGH CARD POINTS THE OPPONENTS HAVE.

2. ON THIS HAND YOU HAVE 23 SO THEY HAVE 17. YOU KNOW THAT EAST MUST HAVE AT LEAST THIRTEEN, SO WEST CAN HAVE NO MORE THAN FOUR. BECAUSE OF THIS REASONING, YOU CAN CONCLUDE THAT WEST DOES NOT HAVE BOTH THE ACE AND KING OF SPADES. BESIDES, IF WEST HAD THOSE CARDS, HE WOULD HAVE DOUBLED 3NT.

3. THIS SPADE COMBINATION IS WORTHY OF STUDY. HAD EAST PLAYED THE ♠ K AND RETURNED THE ♠ J AT TRICK TWO, YOU COULD STILL SHUT OUT FOUR SPADE TRICKS BY DUCKING. IF YOU COVER, WEST WILL DUCK AND YOU WILL LOSE FOUR SPADE TRICKS AGAIN.

(7) DOUBLE FINESSE?

East-West vulnerable
Dealer North

North
♠ Q J 3
♡ A Q 8 7
◇ K 6
♣ J 10 9 2

South
♠ 6 4 2
♡ K J 10 9
◇ A J 3
♣ A 8 7

North	East	South	West
1 ♣	Pass	1 ♡	Dbl.
2 ♡	Pass	4 ♡	All Pass

Opening Lead:　♠ A　(A from AK)

West continues with the king and a spade, East following with the five, seven, ten.

You draw two rounds of trumps with the king and ace, both following. How do you continue?

DOUBLE FINESSE? (SOLUTION)

North
♠ Q J 3
♡ A Q 8 7
◇ K 6
♣ J 10 9 2

West
♠ A K 9 8
♡ 3 2
◇ Q 10 7 5
♣ K Q 4

East
♠ 10 7 5
♡ 6 5 4
◇ 9 8 4 2
♣ 6 5 3

South
♠ 6 4 2
♡ K J 10 9
◇ A J 3
♣ A 8 7

Play king, ace and ruff a diamond, and run the ♣ J. If West does not have the remaining trump he will be endplayed in three suits. (A diamond or a spade will give you a ruff and a sluff, a club will eliminate the second club finesse.)

KEY LESSON POINTERS

1. ALL THE TRUMPS DO NOT HAVE TO BE DRAWN TO STRIP A HAND.
2. IF THE PLAYER BEING THROWN IN (WEST) DOES NOT HAVE THE REMAINING TRUMP, THE EFFECT IS USUALLY THE SAME AS A COMPLETE STRIP.
3. A PLAYER WHO MAKES A TAKEOUT DOUBLE AFTER TWO SUITS HAVE BEEN BID SHOULD HAVE AT LEAST FOUR CARDS IN EACH OF THE UNBID SUITS.
4. AFTER THE BIDDING IS OPENED WITH ONE OF A MINOR AND OPENER RAISES PARTNER'S MAJOR SUIT RESPONSE FROM ONE TO TWO, IT IS IMPORTANT FOR THE DEFENDERS TO KNOW WHETHER OR NOT THIS RAISE PROMISES THREE OR FOUR CARD SUPPORT. ONCE THIS IS KNOWN, IT IS EASIER TO COUNT RESPONDER'S HAND IF THERE IS ANY SUBSEQUENT BIDDING.
FOR EXAMPLE, IF RESPONDER LEAPS TO GAME (AFTER KNOWN FOUR CARD SUPPORT) HE COULD HAVE A FOUR CARD SUIT. IF THE RAISE COULD SHOW THREE, THEN RESPONDER NEEDS A MINIMUM OF FIVE CARDS TO PROCEED IN THE SAME SUIT.

(8) HOW HIGH?

East-West vulnerable
Dealer South

North
♠ J 7 3
♡ 7 3
◇ A K Q J
♣ A 7 4 2

South
♠ 9 6 2
♡ K Q 10 8 4 2
◇ 5 3
♣ K 5

South	West	North	East
2 ♡*	Pass	2 NT	Pass
3 ♣**	Pass	3 ♡	All Pass

*Weak
**Feature

Opening Lead: ♠ K

West continues with the ace and a spade to East's queen. At trick four East produces the one card you don't want to see, the thirteenth spade.

Excluding a 4-1 trump division, what trump holdings will still allow you to make the hand? How do you continue?

HOW HIGH? (SOLUTION)

North
♠ J 7 3
♡ 7 3
♢ A K Q J
♣ A 7 4 2

West
♠ A K 10
♡ 9 6
♢ 8 6 4 2
♣ J 9 6 3

East
♠ Q 8 5 4
♡ A J 5
♢ 10 9 7
♣ Q 10 8

South
♠ 9 6 2
♡ K Q 10 8 4 2
♢ 5 3
♣ K 5

Ruff with the ♡ K. There are technical as well as psychological considerations here.

In order to avoid the loss of two hearts tricks against <u>best defense</u>, you must play East for either J9(x), AJ, or AJx. (We only consider 3-2 heart divisions as a 4-1 division will almost always prove fatal.)

As one of the latter two divisions is more likely than the first, you should ruff high, very high, with the king. Even though you are hoping East has the AJ or AJx of hearts, you should ruff with the king to induce a defensive error. If West has ♡ A9x and overruffs, you can still hold your heart losses to one trick by finessing the ♡ 10 later.

If, when you ruff high, you are not overtrumped, you should cross to dummy and lead a trump toward the ten. If that holds, reenter dummy and lead a second heart.

KEY LESSON POINTERS

1. WHEN THE DEFENSE PUTS YOU IN A POSITION WHERE THERE IS AN OBVIOUS DANGER OF AN OVERRUFF, CONSIDER THE POSSIBLE TRUMP HOLDINGS THAT WILL STILL ALLOW YOU TO MAKE THE HAND AND PLAY FOR ONE OF THEM.
2. ONCE YOU HAVE DECIDED TO RUFF HIGH, RUFF WITH YOUR HIGHEST EQUAL. THIS HAS THE EFFECT OF INDUCING A DEFENSIVE ERROR BY OVERRUFFING. IT WILL USUALLY BE RIGHT FOR THE DEFENDER NOT TO OVERRUFF – BUT NOT EVERY DEFENDER KNOWS THAT.

(9) 4-3-3-3 FACING 4-3-3-3 (2)

Neither side vulnerable
Dealer West

North
♠ A Q 6
♡ A 10 4
◇ Q J 10 9
♣ A Q 10

South
♠ 8 7 5
♡ K Q 9
◇ 5 4 3 2
♣ K 7 6

West	North	East	South
Pass	1 ◇	Pass	1 NT
Pass	3 NT	All Pass	

Opening Lead: ♡ 3

1.   You play low from dummy and win the trick when East plays the ♡ 2. How do you read the heart suit?
2.   At trick two you lead a low diamond. West rises with the ◇ K and switches to the ♠ J. Which spade do you play from dummy? Why?
      You rise with the ♠ A and play a second diamond from dummy.
3.   West wins with the ◇ A and continues with the ♠ 10. Do you cover, or do you play low from dummy?

4-3-3-3 FACING 4-3-3-3 (SOLUTION)

North
♠ A Q 6
♡ A 10 4
◇ Q J 10 9
♣ A Q 10

West
♠ J 10
♡ J 8 6 3
◇ A K 8
♣ 5 4 3 2

East
♠ K 9 4 3 2
♡ 7 5 2
◇ 7 6
♣ J 9 8

South
♠ 8 7 5
♡ K Q 9
◇ 5 4 3 2
♣ K 7 6

1. East should have three small hearts.
2. You only need one spade trick to make your game so you should rise with the ♠ A keeping a second stopper in spades in case East has the ◇ A.
3. Play low. East is marked with the ♠ K on the bidding. West passed originally and has already turned up with 9 high card points. He is not likely to have the ♠ K.

   True, by covering, you might block the suit if West started with specifically ♠ J 10 9. However, with that holding West might have opted to lead a spade originally rather than a heart from Jxxx.

   It is slightly better to play West for ♠ J 10 – besides, that's what he has!

KEY LESSON POINTERS

1. HOLDING xxx IN THE SUIT PARTNER HAS LED AT NOTRUMP, THIRD HAND SHOULD NOT PLAY HIGH. IF THE HIGHEST CARD IS AN EIGHT OR LOWER, THIRD HAND SHOULD SIMPLY GIVE COUNT BY PLAYING LOW.
2. HOLDING AQx FACING xxx, DECLARER CAN FREQUENTLY RETAIN A SECOND STOP IN THE SUIT BY PLAYING THE ACE THE FIRST TIME THE SUIT IS LED. FOR EXAMPLE, ON THIS HAND IF EAST HAS THE SECOND DIAMOND HONOR, DECLARER RETAINS A SPADE STOPPER.
3. PAY ATTENTION TO THE HIGH CARDS THAT STREAM OUT OF AN OPPONENT'S HAND – PARTICULARLY IF HE HAS PASSED ORIGINALLY. ASSUME A PLAYER WHO HAS PASSED ORIGINALLY HAS LESS THAN 12 HIGH CARD POINTS.
4. GIVEN TWO UNBID MAJOR SUITS, MOST DEFENDERS WOULD OPT TO LEAD FROM A STRONG THREE CARD SEQUENCE AS OPPOSED TO Jxxx.

(10) REPRIEVE (1)

Both sides vulnerable
Dealer West

> ### North
> ♠ 9 4
> ♡ 10 9 8
> ◇ A Q J 10 7 6
> ♣ K 5
>
> ### South
> ♠ A K 10
> ♡ A 7 5
> ◇ 8 4 3 2
> ♣ Q J 9

West	North	East	South
1 ♠	2 ◇	Pass	3 NT
All Pass			

Opening Lead: ♡ K (Asks for an unblock or count)

East plays the ♡ 3 and you duck the trick. West continues with the ♡ J and east plays the ♡ 2.
1. What do you do?
    You win the trick and take the diamond finesse.
2. It loses and back comes the ♠ 8.
    What is your plan?

REPRIEVE (SOLUTION)

North
♠ 9 4
♡ 10 9 8
◊ A Q J 10 7 6
♣ K 5

West
♠ Q J 7 6 5
♡ K Q J 6 4
◊ 9
♣ A 2

East
♠ 8 3 2
♡ 3 2
◊ K 5
♣ 10 8 7 6 4 3

South
♠ A K 10
♡ A 7 5
◊ 8 4 3 2
♣ Q J 9

2. It appears that you have been given a reprieve. If East has a doubleton heart and West the club ace, the opponents could have defeated you with a club return.

There is a slim possibility that the hearts are blocked; West might have started with KQJ blank. In that case all you have to do is knock out the ♣ A. However, if West started with ♡ K Q J, East would have started with 6432 and would not be signaling properly to show four cards.

In any case it must be right to run off five more rounds of diamonds, discarding a heart and a club. This will reduce all hands to four cards.

On the discards you will be able to tell whether those hearts are blocked or whether West started with five. West must reduce to four cards. If he elects to save two spades, the ♣ A and the ♡ Q, he will have discarded two hearts. It is now safe to knock out the ♣ A.

If West reduces to two hearts, the ♣ A and a spade honor, you can drop his remaining spade honor by leading a spade from dummy to your ace or king.

If West never discards a heart, but instead discards three clubs and two spades on the diamonds, you know that West cannot have room in his hand for five hearts and the suit must be blocked. Again it is safe to lead a club.

KEY LESSON POINTERS

1. SOME PLAYERS REVERSE THE MEANING OF THE LEAD OF THE ACE AND KING VS. NO TRUMP. THESE PLAYERS LEAD THE ACE FROM WEAKER HOLDINGS SUCH AS AKx(x) AND THE KING FROM ALL STRONG HOLDINGS SUCH AS K Q J(x)(x) OR AKJ10(x).

2. WHEN YOU GIVE COUNT WITH FOUR SMALL, THE PROPER CARD TO PLAY IS SECOND HIGHEST, RESERVING THE HIGHEST FOR DOUBLETONS. IN TRUTH, MOST OF THE TIME IT DOESN'T MATTER WHETHER YOU PLAY HIGHEST OR SECOND HIGHEST FROM FOUR SMALL. HOWEVER, WITH SOMETHING LIKE 10876, IT IS IMPORTANT TO PLAY THE EIGHT AND NOT THE SEVEN.
3. A PLAYER HOLDING GOODIES IN THREE SUITS CAN ALMOST ALWAYS BE SQUEEZED OUT OF ONE TRICK ON THE RUN OF A LONG SUIT. JUST WATCH HIS DISCARDS.

(11) IF AT FIRST.... (1) (2)

North-South vulnerable
Dealer North

> **North**
> ♠ 3 2
> ♡ K 8 7 6 5
> ♢ K 10 9 5
> ♣ A 9

> **South**
> ♠ A Q 6
> ♡ A 10 9 3
> ♢ A 8 6 3
> ♣ 7 5

North	East	South	West
Pass	Pass	1 ♡	Dbl.
4 ♡	Pass	Pass	Pass

Opening Lead: ♣ K

1. Do you take this trick? If not, why not?
   You duck the trick to prevent East from getting the lead later in clubs.
2. West continues with a low club, East playing high-low. What is your next play? Why?
   You play the ♡ K hoping to drop a singleton heart honor in the doubler's hand.
3. All follow low under the ♡ K. When you lead a heart to the ace, West discards a club. Now what?

IF AT FIRST... (SOLUTION)

North
♠ 3 2
♡ K 8 7 6 5
◇ K 10 9 5
♣ A 9

West
♠ K J 5 4
♡ 2
◇ Q J 4
♣ K Q 10 6 2

East
♠ 10 9 8 7
♡ Q J 4
◇ 7 2
♣ J 8 4 3

South
♠ A Q 6
♡ A 10 9 3
◇ A 8 6 3
♣ 7 5

3. At this point you should play ace, king and a diamond hoping that <u>West</u> takes the trick. If he does, and he does not have a fourth diamond with which to exit, he will be forced to lead a black card. Once he does that, you do not lose a spade trick.

KEY LESSON POINTERS

1. WHEN THE KING IS LED VS. A SUIT CONTRACT AND YOU HAVE Ax FACING xx OR Axx FACING xx, AND YOU DO NOT WANT YOUR RIGHT HAND OPPO-NENT ON LEAD LATER IN THE HAND, DUCK THE OPENING LEAD. HERE, YOU WOULD RATHER EAST DID NOT GET IN WITH A CLUB TO LEAD A SPADE.
2. PLAY THE TAKEOUT DOUBLER FOR THE SHORTER HOLDING IN THE TRUMP SUIT.
3. WHEN YOU CAN GIVE UP THE LEAD TO EITHER OPPONENT, THROW IN THE PLAYER WHO CANNOT HURT YOU. FOR EXAMPLE, HERE YOU CAN EI-THER THROW EAST IN WITH A TRUMP OR WEST IN WITH A DIAMOND. BET-TER TO THROW WEST IN BECAUSE OF THE SPADE POSITION.
NOTICE THAT IF YOU WIN THE FIRST CLUB, WEST CAN UNDERLEAD HIS QUEEN OF CLUBS TO EAST'S JACK AFTER BEING THROWN IN WITH A DIA-MOND. EAST THEN SHIFTS TO A SPADE AND THE DEFENDERS TAKE ONE TRICK IN EACH SUIT.

(12) BLACK CITY (1)

North-South vulnerable
Dealer West

North
♠ A K 9 7 5 4
♡ 3
♢ A
♣ Q 10 6 5 4

South
♠ 2
♡ A 9 7 4
♢ Q J 10 9 7 6
♣ A 3

West	North	East	South
3 ♡	3 ♠	Pass	3 NT
All Pass			

Opening Lead: ♡ K

1.   East plays the ♡ 8. Do you take this trick? If so, how do you continue?
       You duck the trick.
2.   West continues with the ♡ 10, East discarding a low diamond. Plan the play.

BLACK CITY (SOLUTION)

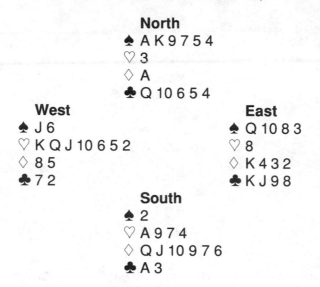

North
♠ A K 9 7 5 4
♡ 3
◇ A
♣ Q 10 6 5 4

West
♠ J 6
♡ K Q J 10 6 5 2
◇ 8 5
♣ 7 2

East
♠ Q 10 8 3
♡ 8
◇ K 4 3 2
♣ K J 9 8

South
♠ 2
♡ A 9 7 4
◇ Q J 10 9 7 6
♣ A 3

2.   Your best shot is to discard the ◇ A on the second round of hearts and drive out the ◇ K. If East has that card, your worries are over; if West has that card, well, you've been down before.

KEY LESSON POINTERS

1. SOMETIMES THE OPPONENTS MUST DO FOR YOU WHAT YOU CANNOT DO FOR YOURSELF. YOU MUST DUCK THE HEART SO THAT YOU CAN UN-BLOCK THE ◇ A ON THE SECOND HEART.
2. WHEN YOU HAVE A CHOICE OF SUITS TO DEVELOP, TRY TO WORK WITH THE SUIT THAT NEEDS THE LEAST GOOD FORTUNE TO BE DEVELOPED. IN THIS HAND YOU HAVE A CHOICE OF THREE SUITS TO ESTABLISH, BUT DIAMONDS IS CLEARLY THE BEST – PROVIDING YOU JETTISON YOUR ACE.
3. SOME PLAYERS ARE INCAPABLE OF UNBLOCKING AN ACE. LET'S HOPE YOU'RE NOT ONE OF THEM.

(13) SHOW OFF (1) (2)

Both sides vulnerable
Dealer South

North
♠ Q 10
♡ 4 3 2
◇ A J 10 9 8 2
♣ 10 2

South
♠ A K
♡ A 10 9 8
◇ K 3
♣ A Q 7 6 5

South	West	North	East
1 ♣	Pass	1 ◇	Pass
2 ♡	Pass	3 ◇	Pass
3 NT	All Pass		

Opening Lead: ♠ 2 (Fourth best)

1. What do you play at trick two? Why?
    You lead a <u>low</u> diamond to the jack. You are hoping that the jack loses to the queen so that you can later overtake the ◇ K. Also, if West has the doubleton queen you are still in great shape.
2. Alas, the ◇ J holds. Now what?
    You throw the ◇ K under the ◇ A and continue with the ◇ 10 discarding your remaining spade honor. Now, at least, the opponents can no longer lead spades.
    When you do this, East wins the ◇ Q and West sheds a spade on the third diamond.
    East leads the ♡ K which you duck; you win the continuation of the ♡ Q. When you exit a heart, East wins the ♡ J and West follows.
3. East exits with the ♣ 9. In your hand at this point are your original five clubs and a winning heart. In dummy are the high spade, three winning diamonds and the ♣ 10 2.
    Which club do you play from your hand?

SHOW OFF (SOLUTION)

North
♠ Q 10
♡ 4 3 2
♢ A J 10 9 8 2
♣ 10 2

West
♠ J 8 3 2
♡ 7 6 5
♢ 7 6
♣ K 8 4 3

East
♠ 9 7 6 5 4
♡ K Q J
♢ Q 5 4
♣ J 9

South
♠ A K
♡ A 10 9 8
♢ K 3
♣ A Q 7 6 5

3. East counts out to exactly two clubs. He can have either 9x, 98, J9, or K9.
    As you cannot make the hand if East has 9x, eliminate that combination from your thinking.
    If East has 98, you must play low, or the queen and then low.
    If East has J9, you must play the ace and then low.
    If East has K9, you must either play ace and then low, or the queen and then low.
    So, the queen and then low wins in two cases and the ace and then low wins in two cases, but playing low wins in only one case.
    However, if East had ♣ 9 8 he might have switched to a club after the first heart held. A strong East would realize that his partner needed two club honors and would have wanted to lead the suit through twice.
    All in all, the ace and then low is slightly the better play.

KEY LESSON POINTERS

1. WHEN A DEFENDER CAN HAVE ONE OF SEVERAL HOLDINGS, ELIMINATE THE ONES THAT DO NOT ALLOW YOU TO MAKE THE HAND AND PROCEED FROM THERE.
2. WITH Kx FACING AJ109xx AND NO SIDE DUMMY ENTRY, LEADING LOW TO THE JACK HAS INTERESTING POSSIBILITIES. IF FOURTH HAND TAKES THE TRICK, OR IF EITHER HAND HAS Qx YOU CAN BRING IN THE SUIT FOR AT LEAST FIVE TRICKS.
3. WITH Qx FACING AK IN A NOTRUMP CONTRACT, IF, AFTER THE SUIT IS LED, YOU UNBLOCK THE REMAINING HONOR FROM THE AK SIDE, YOU CAN EITHER FORCE THE OPPONENTS TO GIVE YOU A TRICK WITH THE Q, OR PREVENT THEM FROM THE LEADING THE SUIT ALTOGETHER.
4. IT PAYS TO KNOW YOUR OPPONENTS' SKILL LEVEL. FOR EXAMPLE, WOULD ANY EAST YOU KNOW BE CAPABLE OF LEADING THE 9 FROM EITHER J9 OR K9 DOUBLETON IN THE END GAME?
    ALSO, HOW LONG DID IT TAKE EAST TO DECIDE ON WHICH CLUB TO LEAD?

(14) EAGLE EYE (1)

East-West vulnerable
Dealer North

North
♠ 5 2
♡ A K J
◇ 4 3
♣ A J 10 9 8 7

South
♠ A J 8 7 4
♡ Q 7 4
◇ A J 7
♣ 6 5

North	East	South	West
1 ♣	Pass	1 ♠	Pass
2 ♣	Pass	2 NT	Pass
3 NT	All Pass		

Opening Lead: ◇ 6

1.   East plays the ◇ Q. Do you win this trick, or do you duck?
     You duck the trick.
2.   East returns the ◇ 2. Do you win this trick or do you play the ◇ J? What is your plan?

EAGLE EYE (SOLUTION)

North
♠ 5 2
♡ A K J
◇ 4 3
♣ A J 10 9 8 7

West
♠ K 9 3
♡ 10 5 2
◇ K 10 8 6
♣ Q 3 2

East
♠ Q 10 6
♡ 9 8 6 3
◇ Q 9 5 2
♣ K 4

South
♠ A J 8 7 4
♡ Q 7 4
◇ A J 7
♣ 6 5

2.   This time you should win the trick. East's return of the ◇ 2 indicates an original holding of either two or four cards.

In either case it is safe to win the trick and start the clubs. If East has four diamonds, the most the defenders can take will be three diamonds and a club (providing you only have one club loser).

If East has no more diamonds you will take his spade shift with the ace and repeat the club finesse.

Notice that if you duck the second diamond, West can shift to a spade, his proper play, and defeat the contract even though the clubs come home.

KEY LESSON POINTERS

1. IF YOU CANNOT TELL HOW AN ADVERSE SUIT IS DIVIDED FROM THE SPOT CARD THAT IS LED, YOU CAN USUALLY TELL HOW IT IS DIVIDED FROM THE SPOT CARD THAT IS RETURNED.
2. KEEP IN MIND THAT DEFENDERS WILL NORMALLY GIVE THEIR PARTNER COUNT AFTER PLAYING THIRD HAND HIGH. WITH TWO REMAINING CARDS THE HIGHER ONE IS RETURNED AND WITH THREE, THE LOWEST.
3. WHEN THERE IS NO DANGER THAT YOU CAN BE DEFEATED IN THE SUIT THAT HAS BEEN LED, BUT THERE IS A DANGER THAT YOU CAN BE DEFEATED WITH A SHIFT, A HOLD-UP PLAY IN THE FIRST SUIT IS NOT EXACTLY VERY CLEVER.
4. ONCE YOU CAN DETERMINE THAT AN ADVERSE SUIT IS DIVIDED EVENLY BETWEEN THE DEFENDERS' HANDS, THERE IS LITTLE REASON TO HOLD UP.
5. HAD EAST RETURNED A HIGH DIAMOND, INDICATING A THREE CARD HOLDING, YOU WOULD HAVE HAD TO HOLD UP UNTIL THE THIRD ROUND OF THE SUIT, RISKING A SPADE SHIFT FROM WEST.

(15) TAKE ME BACK TO THREE NOTRUMP

East-West vulnerable
Dealer South

> ### North
> ♠ 4 2
> ♡ K J 10 6 4
> ◇ 9 6 4
> ♣ 4 3 2
>
> ### South
> ♠ A K 5
> ♡ A Q 9
> ◇ J 10 8
> ♣ A K 8 7

South	West	North	East
2 NT	Pass	3 ◇*	Pass
3 ♡	Pass	3 NT	Pass
4 ♡	All Pass		

*Transfer

Opening Lead: ♠ Q

East plays the ♠ 3. What is your plan?

TAKE ME BACK TO THREE NOTRUMP (SOLUTION)

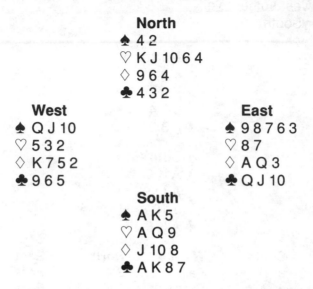

North
♠ 4 2
♡ K J 10 6 4
◇ 9 6 4
♣ 4 3 2

West
♠ Q J 10
♡ 5 3 2
◇ K 7 5 2
♣ 9 6 5

East
♠ 9 8 7 6 3
♡ 8 7
◇ A Q 3
♣ Q J 10

South
♠ A K 5
♡ A Q 9
◇ J 10 8
♣ A K 8 7

Things don't look too rosy, but you have a chance if you duck the opening lead!

If the suit is returned (or the opponents fail to find the diamond shift), you can discard a club from dummy on your extra spade winner and then play ace-king and ruff a club. If clubs divide 3-3, you will be able to discard a diamond loser on your thirteenth club after drawing trumps. How sneaky can you get?

KEY LESSON POINTERS

1. PLAN THE PLAY BEFORE PLAYING A CARD FROM DUMMY. DECEPTIVE PLAYS LOSE QUITE A BIT IN TRANSLATION IF YOU HAVE TO HESITATE BEFORE PLAYING FROM YOUR HAND. THE IDEA IS TO PLAY IN TEMPO.

2. DECEPTIVE PLAYS ARE MOST EFFECTIVE WHEN MADE EARLY IN THE HAND BEFORE THE OPPONENTS CAN COUNT YOUR POINTS AND DISTRIBUTION AND BEFORE THEY CAN SIGNAL ONE ANOTHER.

3. A SELDOM USED PLOY IS DUCKING THE OPENING LEAD IN A SUIT CONTRACT HOLDING xx FACING AKx. OPPONENTS SIMPLY WILL NOT BE EXPECTING IT. ACTUALLY ALL YOU HAVE DONE IS EXCHANGED A CLUB LOSER FOR A SPADE LOSER, GIVING YOURSELF THE OPPORTUNITY TO SET UP A LONG CLUB BEFORE THE OPPONENTS CAN GAUGE YOUR INTENTIONS. HOW CLEVER YOU ARE.

(16) NICE CONTRACT (1)

East-West vulnerable
Dealer East

North
♠ J 3 2
♡ 4 2
◇ A K J 8 7 6 5
♣ 4

South
♠ K 5
♡ A Q J 10 9 8 5
◇ 4 3
♣ A 6

East	South	West	North
Pass	1 ♡	Pass	2 ◇
Pass	3 ♡	Pass	4 ♡

Opening Lead: ♣ J   (Jack denies)

You win the ♣ A and ruff a club in dummy.
1.   How do you continue?
    You cash the ◇ A and play the ace and queen of hearts.
2.   East wins the ♡ K, West discarding a club, and shifts to
a low spade. Do you think you have played the hand
properly up to this point? Which spade do you play from
your hand?

NICE CONTRACT (SOLUTION)

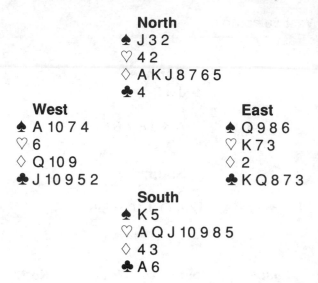

North
♠ J 3 2
♡ 4 2
◇ A K J 8 7 6 5
♣ 4

West
♠ A 10 7 4
♡ 6
◇ Q 10 9
♣ J 10 9 5 2

East
♠ Q 9 8 6
♡ K 7 3
◇ 2
♣ K Q 8 7 3

South
♠ K 5
♡ A Q J 10 9 8 5
◇ 4 3
♣ A 6

2.   You have played the hand properly up to this point.   If hearts had been 2-2 you would be cold. Only if East has ♡ Kxx with a singleton diamond can you have any trouble. However, because you cashed the ◇ A before playing trumps you are still going to make the hand if East has the ♠ Q.

The best East can do is lead a low spade. However, you know that East cannot have the ♠ A because he has already turned up with a marriage in clubs along with the ♡ K. If he had the ♠ A as well, he would have opened the bidding. So duck the spade to West's ace, and let East ruff a diamond. You lose only three tricks.

In case you are wondering why you cashed a diamond early, consider what happens if you play AQ of hearts without cashing the diamond. East wins and plays a diamond and now you cannot get off dummy without losing three more tricks.

What about taking the heart finesse at trick three? Fine on this hand, but if West has the ♡ K and there is a singleton diamond floating around, you are going to be in serious trouble if West shifts to a diamond.   Also, cashing the ◇ A before finessing the heart isn't too clever either. West may give East a diamond ruff and after a club exit you have to lose two spades regardless.

KEY LESSON POINTERS

1. WHEN A CONTRACT LOOKS REASONABLY SECURE GET RID OF THE TRUMPS AS QUICKLY AS POSSIBLE.
2. WHEN THE GRAVEST DANGER TO THE CONTRACT IS THE FEAR OF LOSING A TRUMP TRICK AND THEN BEING PINNED IN DUMMY BY A SINGLETON SWITCH TO A LONG SIDE SUIT, CASH ONE WINNER IN THE SIDE SUIT BEFORE PLAYING TRUMPS.
3. WHEN A PASSED HAND TURNS UP WITH EIGHT HIGH CARD POINTS IN TWO SUITS, ANY MISSING ACE WILL BE IN THE PARTNER'S HAND — UNLESS YOU ARE PLAYING AGAINST CASPER MILQUETOAST.

(17) MICHAELS CUE BID (1) (2)

Neither side vulnerable
Dealer South

North
♠ 2
♡ Q J 8 6
◇ A 4 3 2
♣ J 6 4 3

South
♠ A J 10
♡ A K 10 9 7 3
◇ 7 6 5
♣ Q

South	West	North	East
1 ♡	2 ♡*	4 ♡	4 ♠
5 ♡	All Pass		

* At Least 5-5 with spades and a minor

Opening Lead: ♠ 7   East plays the ♠ Q
                        which you win.

1.   Who has the ♠ K, and what is your next play?
      West should have the ♠ K; the rule of 11 tells you. You
lead the ♠ J which is covered and ruffed in dummy.
2.   Now what? Why?
      You lead a low club toward your blank queen. West's
second suit is surely clubs and he does not have both the
♣ A K or else he would have led the suit. Therefore, East
probably has three clubs to a high honor. If East plays low
you will be able to ruff out East's honor and discard a
diamond on the established ♣ J. No luck. East rises with
the ♣ K, and plays the ◇ Q, West following with the ◇ K.
3.   Do you have any more chances? What is your plan?

MICHAELS CUE BID (SOLUTION)

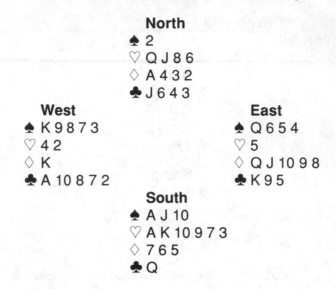

North
♠ 2
♡ Q J 8 6
◊ A 4 3 2
♣ J 6 4 3

West
♠ K 9 8 7 3
♡ 4 2
◊ K
♣ A 10 8 7 2

East
♠ Q 6 5 4
♡ 5
◊ Q J 10 9 8
♣ K 9 5

South
♠ A J 10
♡ A K 10 9 7 3
◊ 7 6 5
♣ Q

3.   You're not dead yet! Win the ◊ A and ruff a club high, reenter dummy with a trump and ruff another club high. Assuming the ♣ A has not appeared, cash the ♠ 10, discarding a diamond, enter dummy with a trump and lead the ♣ J, discarding a diamond.

    If all goes according to plan, West will win the trick. If he does not have a second diamond with which to exit, he will have to lead a black card giving you a ruff and a sluff. You will be able to ruff in dummy and discard your remaining diamond. How nice.

KEY LESSON POINTERS

1. USE THE RULE OF 11 TO LOCATE MISSING HONORS. IT WORKS!
2. EVEN THOUGH YOU MAY NOT KNOW FOR SURE WHO HAS THE ♠ K, AND YOU MAY BE PLANNING ON TRUMPING THE ♠J, BE SURE TO LEAD THE HIGHER OF EQUAL HONORS. IT ENCOURAGES A COVER AND MAKES LIFE SO MUCH EASIER.
3. LEADING TOWARD THE CLOSED HAND IS FAR MORE DECEPTIVE THAN LEADING FROM THE CLOSED HAND – WHEN THE CLOSED HAND HAS A SINGLETON HONOR.
4. WHEN A DEFENDER TIPS OFF HIS DISTRIBUTION DURING THE BIDDING, USE THAT INFORMATION TO GUIDE YOU IN THE PLAY.
5. AT THE POINT THAT WEST PLAYED THE ◊ K, HE COULD CONCEIVABLY HAVE EITHER TWO DIAMONDS AND ONE HEART OR ONE DIAMOND AND TWO HEARTS. AS THE HAND CANNOT BE MADE IF HE HAS TWO DIA-MONDS, ASSUME ONE.

(18) MARGINAL SLAM

North-South vulnerable
Dealer North

North
♠ K Q 7 6
♡ A 8
◇ A K 10 5
♣ J 5 4

South
♠ 5 3 2
♡ Q
◇ 8 4 3
♣ A K Q 10 8 3

North	East	South	West
1 NT	3 ♡	4 ♣	Pass
4 ♡	Pass	6 ♣	All Pass

Opening lead: ♡ 6

You win in dummy and cross to your hand with a trump to lead a spade toward dummy. Your queen in dummy wins the trick.

You return to your hand with a trump, all following, and lead a second spade toward your king, the king also winning. Now what?

MARGINAL SLAM (SOLUTION)

North
♠ K Q 7 6
♡ A 8
♢ A K 10 5
♣ J 5 4

West
♠ A J 10 4
♡ 9 7 6
♢ J 9 7 2
♣ 9 2

East
♠ 9 8
♡ K J 10 5 4 3 2
♢ Q 6
♣ 7 6

South
♠ 5 3 2
♡ Q
♢ 8 4 3
♣ A K Q 10 8 3

Lead dummy's heart and discard your spade. Assume the opponents win and shift to a diamond. You win in dummy and ruff a spade. If spades are 3-3, you can discard your losing diamond on dummy's fourth spade. If West started with four spades your remaining hope is that he started with four or more diamonds. On the run of the clubs the last club will squeeze him between spades and diamonds.

Notice that playing a heart and discarding a spade, with the intention of trumping a spade, is better than leading a spade from dummy after the king wins in the hope the suit is 3-3. If spades are 4-2, West can play a fourth spade and kill any squeeze possibilities.

KEY LESSON POINTERS

1. A JUMP OVERCALL OF A STRONG ONE NOTRUMP OPENING BID IS PRE-EMPTIVE UNLESS THE BIDDER IS VULNERABLE VS. NOT. IN THAT CASE IT IS INVITATIONAL.
2. WHEN YOU ARE TRYING TO ESTABLISH KQxx FACING xxx FOR THREE TRICKS AFTER HAVING WON THE FIRST TWO, IT IS TECHNICALLY MORE ADVANTAGEOUS TO BE ABLE TO DISCARD YOUR REMAINING LOSER ON ANOTHER LOSER AND THEN TRY TO ESTABLISH THE FOURTH CARD BY RUFFING THAN TO PLAY THE SUIT A THIRD TIME. THE DIFFERENCE IS THAT WHEN YOU LEAD THE SUIT A THIRD TIME, A PLAYER WITH FOUR CARDS IN THE SUIT CAN PLAY THE SUIT A FOURTH TIME, DESTROYING ANY SQUEEZE POSSIBILITIES.

(19) A LITTLE LUCK

East-West vulnerable
Dealer North

North
♠ K 4 3 2
♡ K 10 8 7
♢ A K 2
♣ K Q

South
♠ A J 10 8 5
♡ A 3 2
♢ Q J 10
♣ A 6

North	East	South	West
1 ♢	Pass	1 ♠	Pass
3 ♣	Pass	4 NT*	Pass
5 ♡**	Pass	6 ♠	All Pass

* Roman Key Card Blackwood
** Two Key Cards without the queen.

Opening Lead: ♣ J

Your win in dummy and play the king and a spade. On the second round of spades East discards the ♣ 2. Plan the play.

A LITTLE LUCK (SOLUTION)

North
♠ K 4 3 2
♡ K 10 8 7
◇ A K 2
♣ K Q

<table>
<tr><td>West</td><td>East</td></tr>
<tr><td>♠ Q 9 7</td><td>♠ 6</td></tr>
<tr><td>♡ J 4</td><td>♡ Q 9 6 5</td></tr>
<tr><td>◇ 8 7 6</td><td>◇ 9 5 4 3</td></tr>
<tr><td>♣ J 10 9 8 5</td><td>♣ 7 4 3 2</td></tr>
</table>

South
♠ A J 10 8 5
♡ A 3 2
◇ Q J 10
♣ A 6

Your best chance is to win the ♠ A, strip the clubs and diamonds, cash your two hearts, and exit with a spade.

If West started with one or two hearts he will be endplayed. If he started with more than two hearts, tomorrow is another day.

KEY LESSON POINTERS

1. THE HEART SUIT IS INTERESTING. IF DECLARER DOES NOT CASH THE TOP HEARTS BEFORE EXITING A SPADE, HE WILL HAVE TO FIND WEST WITH A VERY SPECIFIC HEART HOLDING TO AVOID THE LOSS OF A TRICK.
2. IF WEST'S ORIGINAL HEART HOLDING IS Jxx OR Qxx, HE CAN EXIT WITH ANY HEART AND COME TO A HEART TRICK. IF HIS ORIGINAL HOLDING IS J9x OR Q9x, HE MUST EXIT WITH AN HONOR. FINALLY, IF WEST START-ED WITH J9xx, Q9xx , OR QJxx , YOU DO HAVE A CHANCE TO AVOID A HEART LOSER, BUT YOU MUST GUESS WHAT TO DO. IN THE FIRST TWO CASES, WEST WILL EXIT WITH AN HONOR AND YOU WILL HAVE TO GUESS TO PLAY EAST FOR HONOR DOUBLETON. WITH QJxx WEST WILL PROBABLY EXIT WITH A LOW HEART, AND YOU WILL HAVE TO BE SMART ENOUGH TO PLAY THE TEN FROM DUMMY.
ALL IN ALL, YOU ARE BETTER OFF TO PLAY WEST FOR A DOUBLETON HEART.

(20) ILLUSION

North-South vulnerable
Dealer North

North
♠ A Q 6
♡ 3 2
◇ Q 5 4
♣ J 10 6 4 3

South
♠ J 10 7 2
♡ K J 9
◇ A K 6
♣ A Q 5

North	East	South	West
Pass	Pass	1 ♣	1 ♡
2 ♣	Pass	2 NT	Pass
3 NT	All Pass		

Opening Lead: ♡ 6

East plays the ♡ 10. Plan the play.

ILLUSION (SOLUTION)

North
♠ A Q 6
♡ 3 2
◊ Q 5 4
♣ J 10 6 4 3

West
♠ 9 5 3
♡ A Q 8 6 5
♡ 10 9 8
♣ K 9

East
♠ K 8 4
♡ 10 7 4
◊ J 7 3 2
♣ 8 7 2

South
♠ J 10 7 2
♡ K J 9
◊ A K 6
♣ A Q 5

You must go to dummy an play the ♣ J, but how should you go over there? Say you go over there with the ◊ Q and the club finesse loses.

You now have nine tricks. . . but you can't take them if West returns a spade. With the club suit blocked you must play low on the spade return. If East has the ♣ K, lights out!

What can you do about this? You might have led a low club to the queen, but that would be silly if East holds ♣ Kxxx. Now you don't have the dummy entries to repeat the finesse.

The better idea is to cross to dummy with the ♠ A and run the ♣ J. If the jack holds, repeat the finesse. If East has ♣ Kxxx,, turn your attention back to spades and knock out the ♠ K.   If East has the ♣ K, West will surely have the ♠ K and you are still in clover.

If West wins the ♣ K (with his actual hand), it is unlikely he will return a spade. He will probably think you have the ♠ K since you crossed to the ♠ A. He is very likely to shift to a diamond. Now you have nine tricks.

Your play of crossing to the ♠ A can only cost you an overtrick; it cannot cost you your contract.

KEY LESSON POINTERS

1. DECLARER MUST ALSO BE AWARE OF WHAT THE OPPONENTS KNOW ABOUT HIS HAND FROM THE BIDDING AND THE PLAY. FOR EXAMPLE, SOUTH KNOWS THAT WEST KNOWS THAT SOUTH HAS AT LEAST THE ♡ K J 9 FROM EAST'S PLAY OF THE ♡ 10 AT TRICK ONE. SOUTH ALSO KNOWS THAT IF HE CROSSES TO THE ◊ Q AT TRICK TWO, WEST WILL KNOW THAT SOUTH STARTED WITH THE ◊ A K. FINALLY, IF WEST HAS THE ♣ K AND READS THE CLUB POSITION, WEST WILL KNOW THAT SOUTH STARTED WITH 17 HIGH CARD POINTS IN CLUBS, DIAMONDS, AND HEARTS AND CANNOT HAVE THE ♠ K OR ELSE HE WOULD HAVE OPENED 2 NT.
    IF ONLY YOUR PARTNERS COULD WORK THINGS LIKE THIS OUT AS EASILY AS YOU!

(21) ROSY OUTLOOK

Neither side vulnerable
Dealer North

North
♠ 9 8 4
♡ K Q 10 9 8
◊ A J 10 6
♣ 8

South
♠ A 3
♡ J
◊ Q 9 3
♣ K Q J 10 9 7 5

North	East	South	West
Pass	Pass	1 ♣	2 ♠*
3 ♡	Pass	3 NT	All Pass
* Weak			

Opening Lead: ♠ Q

East plays the ♠ J at trick one indicating that West has led from a K Q 10 combination and you duck. West continues with the ♠ 10, East following.

How do you place the missing aces, the ◊ K, and what is your plan?

ROSY OUTLOOK (SOLUTION)

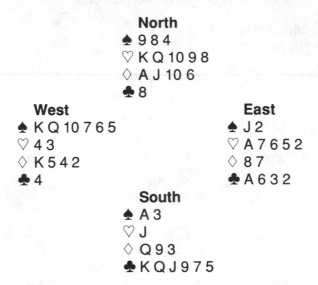

North
♠ 9 8 4
♡ K Q 10 9 8
♢ A J 10 6
♣ 8

West
♠ K Q 10 7 6 5
♡ 4 3
♢ K 5 4 2
♣ 4

East
♠ J 2
♡ A 7 6 5 2
♢ 8 7
♣ A 6 3 2

South
♠ A 3
♡ J
♢ Q 9 3
♣ K Q J 9 7 5

In order to make this hand, East must have both of the missing aces. If this is so, West has the ♢ K because East would have opened the bidding holding two aces, the ♠ J and the ♢ K.

Now that the important cards have been placed, the hand becomes much easier to play. Run the ♢ 9 at trick three. Assuming this holds, run the ♢ Q and then play a third diamond, scoring four diamond tricks in all.

After cashing the diamonds you can exit with any heart or a club. East is down to all hearts and clubs and the very best he can do is cash both aces and throw dummy in with a heart. Eventually West takes the last trick with a spade, but declarer has taken nine tricks.

If you play hearts or clubs before diamonds, East can cash both aces and throw dummy in with a heart. Stuck in the dummy, you can no longer take the diamond finesse or make the hand.

KEY LESSON POINTERS

1. WHEN YOU GET TO A WILDLY OPTIMISTIC UNDOUBLED CONTRACT, PUT THE KEY CARDS WHERE YOU NEED THEM AND PLAY ACCORDINGLY.
2. ASSUME A PLAYER WILL OPEN THE BIDDING WITH 12 HIGH CARD POINTS.
3. HOLDING Q9x FACING AJ10x, RUN THE NINE AND THEN PLAY THE QUEEN AS THE BEST PLAY FOR FOUR TRICKS. THIS IS BETTER THAN PLAYING THE QUEEN FIRST. IF THE QUEEN IS PLAYED FIRST AND IS NOT COVERED, THE SECOND TRICK WILL BE WON BY THE TEN AND A HAND REENTRY IS NEEDED TO REPEAT THE FINESSE A THIRD TIME.

(22) NICE SLAM

Neither side vulnerable
Dealer South

North
♠ A 7
♡ J 6 5
◇ Q 10 8 4
♣ A Q 8 3

South
♠ Q J 9 6
♡ A 3
◇ A K J 7 5 2
♣ 5

South	West	North	East
1 ◇	Pass	2 ♣	Pass
2 ♠	Pass	4 ◇	Pass
4 ♡	Pass	4 ♠	Pass
4 NT*	Pass	5 ♠**	Pass
5 NT	Pass	6 ♣	Pass
6 ◇	All Pass		

* Roman Key Card Blackwood
** 2 Key Cards plus the ◇ Q.

Opening Lead: ♡ 10

You play low from dummy, East plays the ♡ 7 and you win the trick. Both follow when you lay down the ◇ A. How do you continue?

NICE SLAM (SOLUTION)

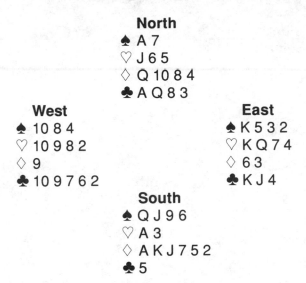

North
♠ A 7
♡ J 6 5
♢ Q 10 8 4
♣ A Q 8 3

West
♠ 10 8 4
♡ 10 9 8 2
♢ 9
♣ 10 9 7 6 2

East
♠ K 5 3 2
♡ K Q 7 4
♢ 6 3
♣ K J 4

South
♠ Q J 9 6
♡ A 3
♢ A K J 7 5 2
♣ 5

You should give yourself two chances to land the slam — either ruffing out the ♣ K or, failing that, taking the spade finesse.

Lead a club to the ace and ruff a club; reenter dummy with a trump and ruff a second club. If no king of clubs has appeared, take the spade finesse.

If the ♣ K makes an early appearance, as it does here, forsake the spade finesse; simply discard your losing heart on the ♣ Q and concede a spade.

KEY LESSON POINTERS

1. WHEN A CONTRACT CAN BE MADE BY ONE OF TWO FINESSES, AND IN ONE OF THE SUITS ESTABLISHMENT BY RUFFING IS POSSIBLE, TRY THAT SUIT FIRST. IF THE CARD YOU ARE LOOKING FOR DOES NOT RUFF OUT, TAKE THE FINESSE IN THE OTHER SUIT.
2. AFTER OPENER REVERSES AND RESPONDER GIVES JUMP PREFERENCE, OPENER FREQUENTLY CUE BIDS AS THIS SEQUENCE SUGGESTS A GOOD POSSIBILITY OF A SLAM.
3. KEY CARD BLACKWOOD IS A VALUABLE SLAM CONVENTION WHEN THERE IS NO CONFUSION AS TO THE AGREED SUIT.

(23) GLOOMY CITY

Neither side vulnerable
Dealer South

North
♠ 7 5
♡ K J 10 6
◇ Q 5 2
♣ A 9 7 6

South
♠ J 4
♡ A Q 9 8 7
◇ A K J
♣ 10 8 4

South	West	North	East
1 ♡	1 ♠	3 ♡	3 ♠
4 ♡	All Pass		

Opening Lead: ♠ K

East signals with the ♠ 9 and West continues with the ♠ 3 to the ♠ A.

East switches to the ◇ 10. Hearts are 2-2 and if you decide to play diamonds, East started with five.

What is your best play?

GLOOMY CITY (SOLUTION)

North
♠ 7 5
♡ K J 10 6
◇ Q 5 2
♣ A 9 7 6

West	East
West	**East**
♠ K Q 10 3 2	♠ A 9 8 6
♡ 3 2	♡ 5 4
◇ 6 4	◇ 10 9 8 7 3
♣ K J 5 2	♣ Q 3

South
♠ J 4
♡ A Q 9 8 7
◇ A K J
♣ 10 8 4

The good news is that the hand can easily be stripped so that if the club suit is blocked (someone has ♣ Kx and doesn't unblock the king under the ace, or either player has KQ, KJ, or QJ doubleton) the hand can still be made.

The bad news is that these holdings are not too likely. Nonetheless, given less than expert defenders, this hand will be made more often than not if the clubs are as you see them.

Your first move after winning the diamond lead in your hand is to lead the ♣ 10 to the ♣ A. Notice that you have no intention of letting the ♣ 10 ride, but psychologically it might induce a cover.

If West covers the ♣ 10 the hand is cold. Simply draw trump, cash the diamonds and exit a club. East will be stuck in with the ♣ Q and will have to give you a ruff and a sluff. Thus you will avoid a second club loser.

Even if West is shrewd enough not to cover the ♣ 10 you can still give him one more problem. Win the ♣ A, draw trump, strip the diamonds ending in your hand and lead a club toward dummy. West must rise with the ♣ K to prevent his partner from being endplayed.

KEY LESSON POINTERS

1. WHEN YOU HAVE LOSERS IN ONLY ONE SUIT, AND THE HAND CAN BE STRIPPED, STRIP THE HAND BEFORE PLAYING THE SUIT WITH THE LOSERS.

2. IF THE SUIT WITH THE LOSERS IS Axxx FACING xxx, IT IS USUALLY RIGHT TO PLAY THE ACE EARLY. A PLAYER HOLDING Kx MAY NOT SEE THE REASON TO UNBLOCK.

3. AFTER CASHING THE ACE AND THEN STRIPPING THE HAND, YOUR SECOND PLAY IN THE SUIT SHOULD FORCE THE PLAYER WITH THE PRESUMED LENGTH TO PLAY SECOND. NOTICE HERE THAT THE SECOND CLUB PLAY COMES FROM THE SOUTH HAND BECAUSE THE CLUB LENGTH IS KNOWN TO BE IN THE WEST HAND. IF WEST REMAINS WITH KJx AND DOES NOT RISE WITH THE KING, EAST, HOLDING A DOUBLETON QUEEN, WILL BE ENDPLAYED.

4. EVEN THOUGH YOU HAVE NO INTENTION OF FINESSING, LEAD THE HIGHEST IN-
    TERMEDIATE CARD YOU HAVE IF YOU WANT A COVER.

(24) DEDUCTIONS (1) (2)

Both sides vulnerable
Dealer West

North
♠ A 10 2
♡ A J 10 3
◇ 10 4
♣ K J 10 6

South
♠ K Q 9 4 3
♡ K Q
◇ 9 6 5 2
♣ 7 3

West	North	East	South
Pass	1 ♣	Pass	1 ♠
Pass	2 ♠	Pass	3 ♠
Pass	4 ♠	All Pass	

Opening Lead: ◇ A (A from AK)

East plays the ◇ Q and West continues with the ◇ 3 to East's ◇ J. At trick three East persists with the ◇ 7. You play low, West plays the ◇ 8 and you ruff low in dummy.

1. What is your general plan?
    You should plan on drawing trumps and discarding two losers on the hearts. A piece of cake.
2. You play the ace and ten of spades to your king, West discarding a low heart. How do you continue with your new "piece of cake"?
    There are two similar approaches, but let's say that you play the ♡ K, overtake the ♡ Q with the ♡ A and play the ♡ J, all following, as you discard the ◇ 9.
3. You lead dummy's fourth heart and East discards a club. How do you play from here? (You remain with ♠ Q 9 4 and ♣ 7 3, dummy has its original four clubs and the good heart that you are leading.)

DEDUCTIONS (SOLUTION)

North
♠ A 10 2
♡ A J 10 3
◇ 10 4
♣ K J 10 6

West
♠ 5
♡ 8 7 5 4
◇ A K 8 3
♣ Q 5 4 2

East
♠ J 8 7 6
♡ 9 6 2
◇ Q J 7
♣ A 9 8

South
♠ K Q 9 4 3
♡ K Q
◇ 9 6 5 2
♣ 7 3

3.   You must ruff your winning heart, reducing yourself to the same trump length as East, and then lead a club to the jack. Assuming East has the ♣ A and West the ♣ Q, East has no answer.

If he ducks the club, you play another club. East must win the ace and lead a spade, allowing you to score the nine and the queen.

If he wins the club and exits a club, you win in dummy and take the last two spade tricks with a trump coup.

KEY LESSON POINTERS

1. IN ORDER TO OPERATE A TRUMP COUP, YOU MUST REDUCE YOURSELF TO THE SAME LENGTH AS YOUR OPPONENT. ASSUMING A TWO CARD ENDING, YOU MUST ARRANGE THAT THE LEAD AT TRICK TWELVE COMES FROM ANYONE BUT YOUR-SELF.

2. AS FAR AS LOCATING THE ♣ A, YOU HAVE SEVERAL CLUES. WEST IS A PASSED HAND AND HAS TURNED UP WITH THE ◇ A K. WITH THE ♣ A HE MIGHT HAVE OPENED. EVEN MORE COMPELLING EVIDENCE IS THAT YOU KNOW WEST'S ORGI-NAL DISTRIBUTION WAS 1-4-4-4 AND HE SURELY WOULD HAVE MADE A PASSED HAND TAKEOUT DOUBLE OF 1 ♠ IF HE HAD THE ♣ A.

3. THIS HAND CANNOT BE MADE IF EAST STARTED WITH THE ♣ A Q, SO YOU SHOULD NOT CONCERN YOURSELF WITH THAT HOLDING.

(25) WHAT A LOVELY DUMMY (1)

East-West vulnerable
Dealer South

              North
              ♠ J 10 7
              ♡ 3 2
              ◊ A K
              ♣ K Q 7 5 3 2

              South
              ♠ A K Q 9 8
              ♡ K J 10 9 8
              ◊ 2
              ♣ A 6

South	West	North	East
1 ♠	Pass	2 ♣	Pass
3 ♡	Pass	3 ♠	Pass
4 ♣	Pass	4 ◊	Pass
4 NT	Pass	5 ◊	Pass
6 ♠	All Pass		

Opening Lead: ◊ Q

1.   You win the ◊ A and lead a spade to the ace, all
following. Now what?
    You cash the ♣ A and lead a low spade to dummy.
2.   How do you continue if spades are 3-2? 4-1?

WHAT A LOVELY DUMMY (SOLUTION)

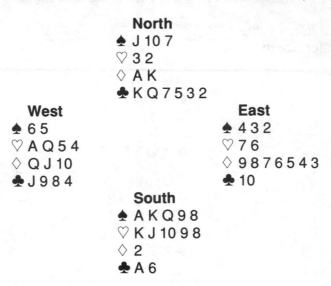

North
♠ J 10 7
♡ 3 2
◇ A K
♣ K Q 7 5 3 2

West
♠ 6 5
♡ A Q 5 4
◇ Q J 10
♣ J 9 8 4

East
♠ 4 3 2
♡ 7 6
◇ 9 8 7 6 5 4 3
♣ 10

South
♠ A K Q 9 8
♡ K J 10 9 8
◇ 2
♣ A 6

2.   If spades are 3-2, play your remaining high diamond and discard the ♣ 6.
Now you can ruff a low club with a high trump, enter dummy with a trump and
discard four of your losing hearts on dummy's clubs. You wind up losing a
heart at the end.

When spades are 3-2, you do not have to risk a favorable club break as
well. You can take out insurance against a 4-1 club division.

When spades are 4-1, you cannot afford the luxury of the club safety
play since you cannot end up in dummy drawing trumps if one opponent has
four.

What you must do is draw the remaining trumps and hope the clubs run.
If they do not, you are going to need some luck in the heart suit. All you can
do after seeing that clubs do not divide is lead a heart to the jack. Against
best defense, you must find East with either a singleton or doubleton queen of
hearts or West with the blank ace.

By leaving both the high club and high diamond in dummy you do give
your opponents a chance to err. If West mistakenly wins the ♡ A holding
Axx, he will have to put you back in dummy for a second heart finesse.

KEY LESSON POINTERS

1.   AT TIMES A LONG SUIT CAN BE ESTABLISHED WITHOUT CASHING TWO ROUNDS OF
THE SUIT. BY DISCARDING ONE AND THEN RUFFING YOU CAN AVOID THE TRAUMA
OF SOMEONE WITH A SINGLETON RUFFING THE SECOND ROUND OF YOUR LONG
SUIT. OF COURSE, YOU MUST HAVE SUFFICIENT ENTRIES TO MAKE THE PLAY.

2.   BY LEAVING BOTH THE HIGH CLUB AND HIGH DIAMOND IN DUMMY (ASSUMING
BOTH BLACK SUITS ARE 4-1) YOU GIVE YOUR LEFT HAND OPPONENT A CHANCE TO
ERR BY WINNING THE ♡ A. HE MUST EITHER RETURN A MINOR SUIT PUTTING YOU
BACK IN DUMMY FOR A SECOND HEART FINESSE OR LEAD A HEART HIMSELF.
WHEN IMMEDIATE DISCARDS DO NOT BENEFIT YOU, DO NOT TAKE THEM.

Section II
DEFENSE

COVER HAND (SOLUTION)

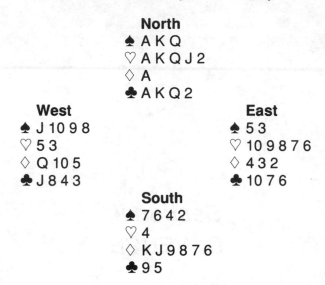

North
♠ A K Q
♡ A K Q J 2
◇ A
♣ A K Q 2

West
♠ J 10 9 8
♡ 5 3
◇ Q 10 5
♣ J 8 4 3

East
♠ 5 3
♡ 10 9 8 7 6
◇ 4 3 2
♣ 10 7 6

South
♠ 7 6 4 2
♡ 4
◇ K J 9 8 7 6
♣ 9 5

You have very little choice. Cash your remaining high cards, the ◇ A and the ♣ A K Q and exit with a low heart from dummy in a two card end position. East will have to win the trick, and if his other card is a diamond you make your ◇ K. If his other card is a club, you have just gone down on a hand in which your partner has presented you with a 32 point dummy!

All's well that ends well. East's other card is a diamond.

(1) CRUDE

Neither side vulnerable
Dealer South

North
♠ A 7 5
♡ 7 2
◇ A K Q 6
♣ J 8 4 2

West (you)
♠ 10 9 8 2
♡ A Q 8 4
◇ 4 2
♣ A 9 7

South	West	North	East
Pass	Pass	1 ◇	Pass
2 NT	Pass	3 NT	All Pass

Opening Lead: ♠ 10

Dummy plays low, partner plays the ♠ Q and declarer wins the trick. At trick two declarer plunks down the ♣ K. Plan your defense.

CRUDE (SOLUTION)

North
♠ A 7 5
♡ 7 2
◇ A K Q 6
♣ J 8 4 2

West
♠ 10 9 8 2
♡ A Q 8 4
◇ 4 2
♣ A 9 7

East
♠ Q 6 3
♡ K 9 6 5
◇ 10 8 5 3
♣ 6 5

South
♠ K J 4
♡ J 10 3
◇ J 9 7
♣ K Q 10 3

Win the ♣ A and shift to a low heart. Declarer is known to have nine winners outside of hearts: three spades, at least three diamonds, and three clubs (he must have the ♣ K Q).

Furthermore, declarer does not need the ♡ K for his passed hand 2NT response. He is already known to have 9 points in the black suits and could have both red jacks to make up the proper count.

KEY LESSON POINTERS

1. WHEN DECLARER PLAYS LOW FROM DUMMY AT TRICK ONE, THE OPENING LEADER WILL USUALLY BE ABLE TO TELL HOW MANY TRICKS DECLARER HAS IN THE SUIT THAT HAS BEEN LED – AFTER SEEING PARTNER PLAY THIRD HAND.
2. WHEN DECLARER LEADS A KING FROM HIS HAND WITH THE JACK ON THE BOARD, ASSUME HE HAS THE QUEEN.
3. WHEN DECLARER IS KNOWN TO HAVE ENOUGH TRICKS TO MAKE HIS CONTRACT IN THREE SUITS, SWITCH TO THE FOURTH – THE WORST THAT CAN HAPPEN IS AN OVERTRICK OR TWO.
4. COUNT DECLARER'S POINTS AS THE PLAY DEVELOPS. ON THIS HAND YOU KNOW NINE OF THE ELEVEN OR TWELVE THAT DECLARER MUST HAVE BY TRICK TWO!

(2) WHO'S CRAZY NOW?

East-West vulnerable
Dealer South

North
♠ Q 10
♡ 6 2
◇ 5 4
♣ A K Q J 9 8 7

                           East (you)
                           ♠ A 9
                           ♡ K 7 5 4 3
                           ◇ 10 3
                           ♣ 10 5 3 2

South	West	North	East
1 ◇	Pass	2 ♣	Pass
3 ◇	Pass	5 ♣	Pass
5 ◇	All Pass		

Opening lead: ♡ J

You play low at trick one and declarer wins the ♡ Q. At trick two declarer leads a low spade to dummy's queen, partner playing the ♠ 2.
1. What do you think declarer's distribution is?
2. How do you plan your defense?

WHO'S CRAZY NOW? (SOLUTION)

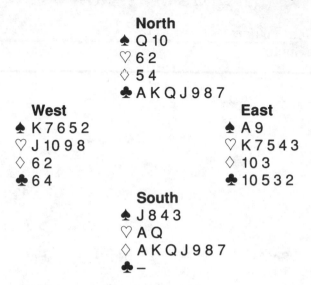

North
♠ Q 10
♡ 6 2
♢ 5 4
♣ A K Q J 9 8 7

West
♠ K 7 6 5 2
♡ J 10 9 8
♢ 6 2
♣ 6 4

East
♠ A 9
♡ K 7 5 4 3
♢ 10 3
♣ 10 5 3 2

South
♠ J 8 4 3
♡ A Q
♢ A K Q J 9 8 7
♣ —

1.   Declarer appears to have four spades as partner's ♠ 2 should be a count signal indicating an odd number of spades, surely five.

Furthermore, North has shown solid clubs so South must have solid diamonds. The only conceivable reason for South to be playing a spade is that he is void in clubs. Therefore declarer must be 4-2-7-0.

2.   Even though they say that when both sides play the same suit, one side is crazy, it must be right to return your remaining spade. If certainly can't hurt, and if partner has the ♠ K you will be able to overtrump the third spade.

True, even if your don't return a spade, declarer may play a second round of the suit before drawing trumps, but why take unnecessary risks?

KEY LESSON POINTERS

1. WHEN DECLARER DOES NOT USE A SOLID SUIT IN THE DUMMY WHEN HE HAS A KNOWN SOLID SUITE IN HIS HAND, ASSUME HE IS VOID IN DUMMY'S SUIT – OR NEEDS A FRONTAL LOBOTOMY.
2. USE PARTNER'S COUNT SIGNALS, THE BIDDING, PLUS THE WAY DECLARER IS ATTACKING THE PLAY TO COUNT THE HAND.

(3) KEEPING COOL

East-West vulnerable
Dealer South

North
♠ A 3 2
♡ A J 9 8 6
◇ A 6 5
♣ K 4

East (you)
♠ 10 7 6 5
♡ 7
◇ Q 3
♣ Q 9 8 7 5 3

South	West	North	East
1 NT	Pass	2 ♣	Pass
2 ♡	Pass	6 ♡	All Pass

Opening lead: ◇ J

Declarer wins the ◇ K and cashes the ♡ A K, as you discard a club and partner follows with the deuce and five.

Next, declarer leads the ♠ Q which partner covers and dummy wins. Declarer follows with the ♣ A and the ♣ J to the ♣ K, partner playing low-high in clubs. Are you still with me? You haven't had to do anything yet — but pay attention!

With the lead in dummy, declarer leads a spade to his jack and partner's four. A diamond is led to the ace, partner playing the ten, and a third spade is led from dummy. Are you ready?

You remain with the ten and a low spade and three clubs. Dummy is leading its last spade and has three trumps and a diamond. Which spade do you play, and why?

KEEPING COOL (SOLUTION)

North
♠ A 3 2
♡ A J 9 8 6
♢ A 6 5
♣ K 4

West
♠ K 9 4
♡ 5 2
♢ J 10 9 8 2
♣ 10 6 2

East
♠ 10 7 6 5
♡ 7
♢ Q 3
♣ Q 9 8 7 5 3

South
♠ Q J 8
♡ K Q 10 4 3
♢ K 7 4
♣ A J

Did you go up with the ♠ 10 because you thought your partner might have the ♡ Q? If you did, don't admit it, think of another reason like the ten slipped out of your hand, or the devil made you do it, or something.

Partner doesn't have the ♡ Q and declarer doesn't have the ♠ 9. If partner has the ♡ Q, declarer started with 14 high card points. Besides, if partner has the ♡ Q, how is declarer going to avoid losing a diamond and a heart even if you duck the spade?

Finally, if declarer had the ♠ 9, why didn't he finesse spades the second time around? You must adjust your thinking to what is actually taking place – even if you don't agree with the bidding.

Declarer is known to have two clubs and three diamonds. (Partner's play of a high card after having first led an honor indicates an odd number of cards.)

If declarer has four hearts and four spades he has no play for the hand regardless of which spade you play, so assume five hearts and three spades. If declarer has five hearts and three spades you must assume your partner has the ♠ 9, otherwise you cannot defeat the contract. You do remember you have no more diamonds at this point, don't you? What are you going to play after winning the ♠ 10 that will not give declarer a ruff and a sluff?

KEY LESSON POINTERS

1. IT IS NOT AGAINST THE LAW TO OPEN ONE NOTRUMP WITH A FIVE CARD MAJOR.
2. WHEN DECLARER HAS A MARKED FINESSE TO TAKE AND DOESN'T TAKE IT (IF DE-CLARER HAD ♠ Q J 9, HE WOULD HAVE FINESSED THE NINE OF SPADES THE SEC-OND TIME THE SUIT WAS PLAYED), ASSUME HE DOESN'T HAVE THOSE CARDS.
3. WHEN YOU NEED YOUR PARTNER TO HAVE A PARTICULAR CARD TO DEFEAT THE CONTRACT (THE ♠ 9), PLAY HIM FOR IT.
4. DON'T FORGET TO CONGRATULATE YOUR PARTNER FOR COVERING THE ♠ Q. IF HE HADN'T, HE WOULD HAVE BEEN THROWN IN WITH THE THIRD DIAMOND AND FORCED TO LEAD AWAY FROM HIS ♠ K. IT IS DANGEROUS TO COVER A QUEEN WITH A KING WHEN DECLARER MIGHT HAVE AQJ9 COMBINATION. HOLDING THE NINE IT IS MUCH SAFER TO COVER.

(4) THE CASE OF THE FATAL DISCARD

Both sides vulnerable
Dealer North

North
♠ Q J 10 9 4 2
♡ A K 2
♢ A 5
♣ 10 6

East (you)
♠ 3
♡ 10 5 4
♢ K 9 6 4 2
♣ Q 8 3 2

North	East	South	West
1 ♠	Pass	2 ♡	Pass
3 ♡	Pass	4 ♣	Pass
4 ♢	Dbl.	4 ♠	Pass
6 ♡	All Pass		

Opening lead: ♢ J

Dummy wins as you signal smartly with the ♢ 6. At trick two declarer crosses to the ♠ A, partner playing the ♠ 5, and plays a heart to dummy, partner following.

At trick four declarer leads the ♠ Q from dummy. What do you discard?

THE CASE OF THE FATAL DISCARD (SOLUTION)

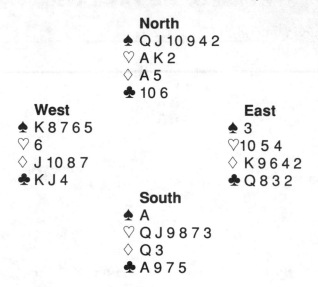

North
- ♠ Q J 10 9 4 2
- ♡ A K 2
- ◇ A 5
- ♣ 10 6

West
- ♠ K 8 7 6 5
- ♡ 6
- ◇ J 10 8 7
- ♣ K J 4

East
- ♠ 3
- ♡ 10 5 4
- ◇ K 9 6 4 2
- ♣ Q 8 3 2

South
- ♠ A
- ♡ Q J 9 8 7 3
- ◇ Q 3
- ♣ A 9 7 5

Surely you must have realized by now that whenever I ask you what you discard, you should trump.

Here is a clear-cut case of killing dummy's long suit by ruffing before declarer can concede a trick to partner's king.

Notice that if you ruff, declarer has nowhere to go. Twist and turn as he might, he must lose a diamond and a club. He simply does not have the entries to set up the spades once you ruff. Exchange the ♡ 2 with the ♡ 3 and declarer can still make the hand by overruffing, crossing to dummy with a trump and leading the ♠ J, discarding a diamond.

However, dummy has the ♡ 2 and you can see that ♡ 2. You can see that you can kill the dummy by ruffing the spade. So kill it!

KEY LESSON POINTERS

1. EVEN THOUGH YOU KNOW THAT PARTNER CAN WIN A TRICK IN A SUIT IN WHICH BOTH YOU AND DECLARER ARE VOID, IT IS FREQUENTLY RIGHT TO RUFF THE TRICK AHEAD OF DECLARER TO PREVENT THE ENTIRE SUIT FROM BEING ESTABLISHED.
2. DON'T FALL ASLEEP DURING THE BIDDING. YOU MAY HAVE A CHANCE TO MAKE A LEAD-DIRECTING DOUBLE OF A CUE BID.

(5) HOW STRANGE! (1) (2)

East-West vulnerable
Dealer South

                    North
                    ♠ A 8 7
                    ♡ K Q 8 3
                    ◇ 8 7
                    ♣ J 10 7 2

West (you)
♠ Q J 10 6 4
♡ 6
◇ Q J 5
♣ 9 6 4 3

South	West	North	East
1 ◇	Pass	1 ♡	Pass
3 ♣	Pass	4 ♣	Pass
4 ♡	Pass	4 ♠	Pass
5 ◇	Pass	6 ♣	All Pass

Opening lead: ♠ Q

Dummy wins, partner flagging with the ♠ 9, and the ♣ J is run from dummy, partner playing low. When a second low club is played from dummy, partner produces the ♣ Q which declarer tops with the ace.

Declarer exits with a low diamond to your jack, partner playing the ◇ 10.

1.   Do you have your senses about? What do you play now?
     You should play a spade in order to force declarer to ruff with his last trump, the king, and promote a probable trump trick for yourself.

2.   Declarer ruffs your spade return and cashes the ◇ A K, partner discarding a low heart on the third round of diamonds. What was declarer's original distribution?
          1-3-6-3.

3.   Declarer continues by playing a fourth high diamond.
     Plan your defense.

HOW STRANGE! (SOLUTION)

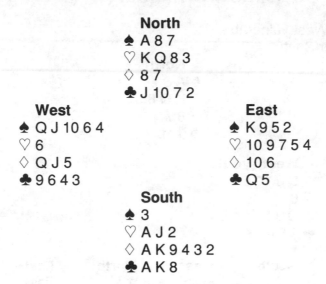

North
♠ A 8 7
♡ K Q 8 3
◇ 8 7
♣ J 10 7 2

West
♠ Q J 10 6 4
♡ 6
◇ Q J 5
♣ 9 6 4 3

East
♠ K 9 5 2
♡ 10 9 7 5 4
◇ 10 6
♣ Q 5

South
♠ 3
♡ A J 2
◇ A K 9 4 3 2
♣ A K 8

3. Discard your heart as if it were a hot potato. Declarer has erred. He should have cashed one heart before running his diamonds. In that way he could have discarded dummy's last spade and the remaining three hearts on the good diamonds, reducing to just two cards and you would be helpless.

    However, now that he has neglected to cash one heart, you have the upper hand. Your best play after discarding the heart is to continue discarding on the diamonds. Eventually declarer will have to lead a heart in a three card end position and you will be able to ruff.

KEY LESSON POINTERS

1. KEEP COUNTING AT ALL TIMES. ON THIS HAND YOU HAD AN EARLY COUNT ON THE TRUMP SUIT. THE BIDDING TOLD YOU THAT SOUTH HAD THREE HEARTS AND PARTNER'S COUNT SIGNAL IN DIAMONDS SHOULD HAVE ENABLED YOU TO COUNT THE ENTIRE HAND AT TRICK FOUR.
2. WHEN DECLARER IS PEELING OFF A LONG SUIT WHICH YOU CAN TRUMP, BUT WHICH WILL BE OVERTRUMPED IN DUMMY, THUS COSTING YOURSELF A TRUMP TRICK, CONSIDER VOIDING YOURSELF IN ANOTHER SUIT. PERHAPS, WHEN DECLARER IS THROUGH RUNNING THE LONG SUIT, YOU WILL BE ABLE TO RUFF THAT SUIT.

(6) THE WEAK NOTRUMP (1) (2) (3) (4)

North-South vulnerable
Dealer East

North
♠ 2
♡ A 8 3 2
♢ 10 9 8 7
♣ A Q J 9

East (you)
♠ K J 5
♡ Q J 10
♢ A Q 3 2
♣ 7 6 5

East	South	West	North
1 NT*	Pass	2 ♠	Dbl.
Pass	3 NT	All Pass	
* 12 - 14			

Opening Lead: ♣ 4

1. How do you play your spades? Why?
    You should start by playing the ♠ J. If partner has the
    ♠ Q, it doesn't matter which honor you play first, nor does
    it matter if declarer has both the ♠ A Q.
    The critical holdings are when declarer has the Q(10)xx
    and partner the ♠ A.
    If partner has led from ♠ A 10 8xx you can take the first
    five tricks in spades if yoiu make the normal play of the king
    followed by the jack. However, you do not need five tricks
    in spades to defeat this contract. Four plus the ♢ A will do
    nicely, thank you.
    What you want is for declarer, holding Q10xx, to win the
    first spade so you can reel off four more spades after
    winning the ♢ A.
2. Your ♠ J holds. What do you play now?
    It can't hurt to continue with the ♠ K, so you do. Your
    king holds, partner playing the ♠ 3, declarer the ♠ 8.
3. Now what?
    Time to shift to the ♡ Q. If you don't know why, stay
    tuned.
4. Declarer wins the ♡ A in dummy and leads the ♢ 10.
    What do you do? You duck the trick and the ten holds.
    Dummy continues with a second diamond to your ace.
    Declarer follows with the ♢ J, and partner also follows.
5. Now what?

THE WEAK NOTRUMP (SOLUTION)

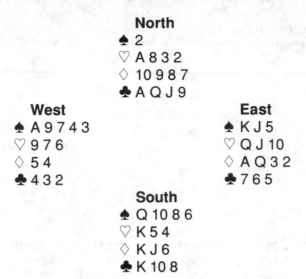

North
♠ 2
♡ A 8 3 2
◇ 10 9 8 7
♣ A Q J 9

West
♠ A 9 7 4 3
♡ 9 7 6
◇ 5 4
♣ 4 3 2

East
♠ K J 5
♡ Q J 10
◇ A Q 3 2
♣ 7 6 5

South
♠ Q 10 8 6
♡ K 5 4
◇ K J 6
♣ K 10 8

5.   Play a second heart. Do not play that last spade. Count declarer's tricks. He has at most two hearts, two diamonds, and four clubs.

If you play a spade you will be setting up his ninth trick in spades before you drive out his other heart stopper.

You must assume partner has the ♠ A to defeat the contract. As it is very likely that declarer started with ♠ Q 10 8x, a third round of spades by you is premature. Establish the setting trick in hearts first. Three spades, one heart and one diamond will defeat three notrump.

KEY LESSON POINTERS

1. ALTHOUGH IT IS USUALLY RIGHT TO PLAY THIRD HAND HIGH HOLDING KJx, OR AJx, THERE ARE EXCEPTIONS. WHEN YOU HAVE ALL OF THE MISSING HIGH CARD STRENGTH YOU WANT TO DISCOURAGE DECLARER FROM HOLDING UP. IF YOU PLAY THE JACK, YOU MAY ENCOURAGE HIM TO TAKE A TRICK IN THE SUIT PREMATURELY. THIS IS THE SAME REASONING ONE USES WITH A Qx IN THE THIRD SEAT. IF YOU PLAY THE QUEEN, DECLARER WILL FREQUENTLY BE FORCED TO TAKE THE TRICK WITH THE KING, NOT KNOWING WHERE THE ACE IS. IF YOU PLAY THE ACE AND THEN THE QUEEN, DECLARER WILL HAVE A MUCH EASIER TIME MAKING A HOLDUP PLAY.

2. KEEP TRACK OF DECLARER'S TRICKS AS THE PLAY DEVELOPS. NOTICE THAT IF YOU WIN THE FIRST DIAMOND LEAD WITH THE ACE YOU WILL NOT BE ABLE TO COUNT DECLARER'S DIAMOND TRICKS BECAUSE YOU WON'T KNOW WHETHER DE-CLARER STARTED WITH THREE OR FOUR DIAMONDS. BY WINNING THE SECOND DIAMOND, YOU KNOW THAT DECLARER CAN ONLY TAKE TWO DIAMOND TRICKS.

3. AS LONG AS YOU KNOW THAT DECLARER CANNOT REEL OFF ENOUGH TRICKS TO MAKE HIS CONTRACT, YOU CAN CONCENTRATE ON ESTABLISHING EXTRA TRICKS FOR YOURSELF (HEARTS) RATHER THAN TRYING TO CASH OUT IN NON-CASH-OUTABLE SUITS (SPADES) ! IS THAT ENGLISH?

(7) NOT SO FAST

East-West vulnerable
Dealer North

North
♠ Q J 3
♡ A Q 8 7
◇ K 6
♣ 9 8 7 6

West (you)
♠ A K 9 8
♡ 2
◇ Q 10 7 5
♣ K Q 4 2

North	East	South	West
1 ♣	Pass	1 ♡	Dbl.
2 ♡	Pass	4 ♡	All Pass

Opening Lead: ♠ A (A from AK)

You continue with the king and a spade, all following. Declarer continues with the king and ace of hearts, partner playing three, four as you discard a club.

Next, declarer plays the king, ace and ruffs the ◇ J, partner playing high-low in diamonds and following to all three rounds.

1. What do you make out the distribution of declarer's hand to be?

2. At this point declarer leads a club from dummy, partner plays the five, and declarer the jack.

   After winning this trick, you remain with a spade, a diamond and king and a club. Dummy has a trump and three clubs. What do you return?

NOT SO FAST (SOLUTION)

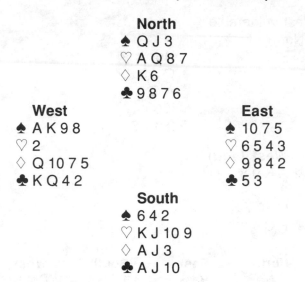

North
♠ Q J 3
♡ A Q 8 7
♢ K 6
♣ 9 8 7 6

West
♠ A K 9 8
♡ 2
♢ Q 10 7 5
♣ K Q 4 2

East
♠ 10 7 5
♡ 6 5 4 3
♢ 9 8 4 2
♣ 5 3

South
♠ 6 4 2
♡ K J 10 9
♢ A J 3
♣ A J 10

1. Declarer is known to have three spades and three diamonds. Partner's high-low in diamonds has shown an even number, obviously four. That leaves declarer seven cards in hearts and clubs.

   If declarer started with six hearts and one club, he would be claiming at this point with a trump flush — so forget that.

   If declarer started with five hearts and two clubs, partner would have started with three clubs and three hearts. He might have high-lowed in hearts to show three; and he would have to hold specifically ♣ A 10 5 to justify his play of the ♣ 5 in the end game.

   Furthermore, if partner has ♣ A 10 5, declarer has leaped to game holding a balanced ten count opposite a single raise.

   No, all the clues point to South having started with 3-4-3-3.

2.. Once you have worked out the distribution, you should be able to work out that it is best to lead your spade, the suit your partner doesn't have. When declarer gleefully trumps in dummy while shedding his losing club, partner will also shed his remaining club. Declarer will not be able to come off dummy without allowing partner to ruff away his ♣ A.

KEY LESSON POINTERS

1. THERE IS NO DEFENSE IF YOU DON'T COUNT. YOU WILL BE GUESSING THE REST OF YOUR LIFE AS TO WHAT TO PLAY.

2. PARTNER CAN HELP YOU OUT ENORMOUSLY ON DEFENSE BY GIVING YOU ACCURATE COUNT SIGNALS WHEN THE OPPONENTS LEAD THE SUIT FIRST. (LOW-HIGH SHOWS AN ORIGINAL ODD NUMBER, HIGH-LOW AN ORGINAL EVEN NUMBER.)

3. MANY PAIRS HAVE ADOPTED UPSIDEDOWN COUNT SIGNALS. THESE PAIRS PLAY THAT LOW-HIGH SHOWS AN ORIGINAL EVEN NUMBER OF CARDS, HIGH-LOW AN ODD NUMBER OF CARDS.

4. WHEN GIVING COUNT IN THE TRUMP SUIT, LOW-HIGH ALWAYS SHOWS AN EVEN NUMBER AND HIGH-LOW AN ODD NUMBER.

(8) IS HE KIDDING?

North-South vulnerable
Dealer South

North
♠ J 7 3
♡ 7 3
◇ A K J 10
♣ A 10 4 2

West (you)
♠ A K 10
♡ K 8 4
◇ Q 9 8 7
♣ K 9 8

South	West	North	East
2 ♡*	Dbl.	Rdbl.	2 ♠
Pass	Pass	3 ♡	Pass
Pass	Pass		
*Weak			

Opening Lead: ♠ K

Partner signals with the ♠ 8 so you continue with the ace and a spade to partner's queen, declarer following. At trick four partner produces the thirteenth spade and declarer ruffs with the ♡ Q. What do you do?

IS HE KIDDING? (SOLUTION)

North
♠ J 7 3
♡ 7 3
◇ A K J 10
♣ A 10 4 2

West	East
♠ A K 10	♠ Q 8 5 4
♡ K 8 4	♡ 10 9
◇ Q 9 8 7	◇ 4 3 2
♣ K 9 8	♣ Q 7 6 3

South
♠ 9 6 2
♡ A Q J 6 5 2
◇ 6 5
♣ J 5

Don't even think of overruffing. Notice that if you don't overtrump you will come to <u>two</u> natural trump tricks, if you overtrump, only one.

KEY LESSON POINTERS

1. DEFENDERS CAN OFTEN PROMOTE EXTRA TRICKS FOR THEMSELVES IN THE TRUMP SUIT BY <u>NOT</u> OVERTRUMPING A DECLARER WHO IS KNOWN TO HAVE A <u>STRONG</u> TRUMP SUIT — PROVIDING THEY CANNOT LOSE THEIR TRUMP TRICK.

North
♠ 3 2

West	East
♠ Q 8 5 4	♠ 9

South
♠ A K J 10 7 6

ASSUME EAST LEADS A CARD THAT NEITHER SOUTH NOR WEST HAS. SPADES ARE TRUMP. WHEN SOUTH RUFFS WITH THE ♠ J, WEST GAINS A TRICK BY <u>NOT</u> OVERTRUMPING.

North
♠ A 3 2

West	East
♠ K 8 4	♠ 7 6

South
♠ Q J 10 9 5

AGAIN EAST LEADS A CARD THAT NEITHER SOUTH NOR WEST HAS, BUT THAT DUMMY HAS. SOUTH RUFFS WITH A QUEEN. THIS TIME WEST DOES BEST TO OVERTRUMP AS HE COULD LOSE HIS KING VIA A LATER FINESSE.
WE DON'T HAVE TO CHANGE THE DIAGRAM POSITION MUCH TO MAKE IT RIGHT FOR WEST NOT TO OVERTRUMP.

North
♠ A 3 2

West	East
♠ K 9 7	♠ 10

South
♠ Q J 8 6 5 4

SAME POSITION, BUT THIS TIME WHEN SOUTH TRUMPS WITH THE QUEEN, WEST GAINS A TRICK BY NOT OVERTRUMPING. WEST CAN AFFORD NOT TO OVERTRUMP BECAUSE HE IS ALREADY ASSURED OF ONE TRUMP TRICK ONCE SOUTH HAS TRUMPED WITH AN HONOR. THE POWER OF THE NINE.

(9) FALSE START (2)

Neither side vulnerable
Dealer West

North
♠ A Q
♡ A 7 5
◇ Q J 10 9 8
♣ A Q 10

West (you)
♠ J 10 5
♡ Q10 8 2
◇ A 6
♣ J 4 3 2

West	North	East	South
Pass	1 ◇	Pass	1 NT
Pass	3 NT	All Pass	

Opening Lead: ♡ 2

Dummy plays low, partner plays the ♡ 3 and declarer wins the ♡ 9.
1. How do you read the heart suit?
2. At trick two declarer leads a low diamond. Which diamond do you play?
   You rise with the ◇ A and play....?
   You shift to the ♠ J.
3. Declarer finesses the queen but partner wins and returns the ♠ 4. Which spade do you play? Why?

FALSE START (SOLUTION)

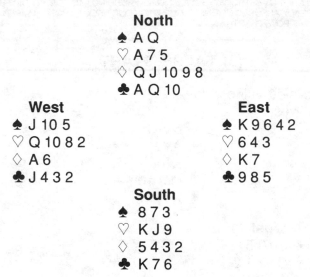

North
♠ A Q
♡ A 7 5
◇ Q J 10 9 8
♣ A Q 10

West
♠ J 10 5
♡ Q 10 8 2
◇ A 6
♣ J 4 3 2

East
♠ K 9 6 4 2
♡ 6 4 3
◇ K 7
♣ 9 8 5

South
♠ 8 7 3
♡ K J 9
◇ 5 4 3 2
♣ K 7 6

1.   Partner has three piglets in hearts. He should not play third hand high with three cards headed by an eight or less. He should give count instead.

3.   Your only chance to defeat this contract is to play partner for the ◇ K (otherwise declarer has nine tricks) and the ♠ 9. If he has those two cards you must unblock the ♠ 10 so that he can run his spades without interruption when he gains the lead with the ◇ K. You have to play this game with a certain degree of optimism.

KEY LESSON POINTERS

1. ONCE YOU REALIZE THAT YOU HAVE NOT LED THE RIGHT SUIT, DON'T GIVE UP, THERE MAY STILL BE TIME TO TRY ANOTHER..

2. WHEN YOU NEED CERTAIN CARDS IN YOUR PARTNER'S HAND TO DEFEAT A CON-TRACT, ASSUME HE HAS THEM AND PLAY ACCORDINGLY.

3. WHEN RETURNING A SUIT PARTNER HAS LED, THE STANDARD RETURN IS YOUR ORIGINAL FOURTH BEST. HOWEVER, TO PREVENT YOUR PARTNER FROM MAKING AN UNFORTUNATE UNBLOCK, YOU SOMETIMES HAVE TO VARY THE RETURN.
   FOR EXAMPLE, IN THIS CASE, EAST WANTS HIS PARTNER TO UNBLOCK THE TEN SO HE RETURNS HIS ORIGINAL FOURTH BEST SPADE. IF EAST'S SPADE HOLDING WERE K8764 HE SHOULD RETURN THE ♠ 8, CONVENIENTLY DENYING THE ♠ 9. WEST WILL NO LONGER UNBLOCK WHEN HE BECOMES AWARE THAT SOUTH HAS THE ♠ 9.

4. ONCE YOU DISCOVER THE HEART POSITION AT TRICK ONE, YOU CAN COUNT NINE TRICKS FOR DECLARER IF DECLARER HAS THE ◇ K. FURTHERMORE, YOU NEED PARTNER TO HOLD THE ♠ K TO HAVE ANY CHANCE. IF PARTNER HAS THESE CARDS THEN DECLARER MUST HAVE THE ♣ K TO JUSTIFY HIS RESPONSE. IF SOUTH HAS THE ♣ K THEN PARTNER NEEDS THE ♠ 9 BESIDES THOSE TWO KINGS WE ARE PLAYING HIM FOR TO DEFEAT THE CONTRACT. I'M SURE YOU THOUGHT OF ALL OF THAT... BUT JUST IN CASE.

(10) BIDS ONE, LEADS ANOTHER (1)

Neither side vulnerable
Dealer West

North
♠ 9 3
♡ 9 8 7 6
◇ A Q J 10 7 6
♣ K

East (you)
♠ 8 4 2
♡ 4 3
◇ K 5
♣ 10 8 6 5 4 3

West	North	East	South
1 ♠	2 ◇	Pass	3 NT
All Pass			

Opening Lead: ♡ K, which holds the trick.

Partner continues with the ♡ 10 and declarer wins the second heart with the ace.

At trick three declarer leads the ◇ 4, partner plays the ◇ 9 and dummy plays the ◇ 10.

1.   Do you take this trick?

Yes. Partner's nine may be a singleton, and wouldn't that be lovely, if you duck and declarer leads the ace?

2.   Having overcome the first hurdle, what do you return at trick four?

BIDS ONE, LEADS ANOTHER (SOLUTION)

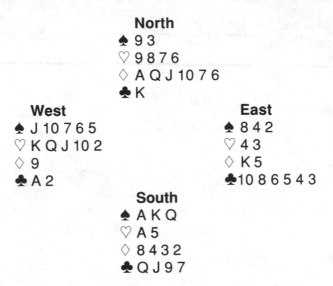

North
♠ 9 3
♡ 9 8 7 6
◇ A Q J 10 7 6
♣ K

West
♠ J 10 7 6 5
♡ K Q J 10 2
◇ 9
♣ A 2

East
♠ 8 4 2
♡ 4 3
◇ K 5
♣ 10 8 6 5 4 3

South
♠ A K Q
♡ A 5
◇ 8 4 3 2
♣ Q J 9 7

2.   A club. Partner had a choice of equal heart honors to play at trick two, and selected his lowest. As that is the only way he can tell you where his side entry is, you should assume that the ♡ 10 is a suit preference play.

If you trust your partner, you will return a club. A spade return at this point is an unspeakable insult.

Nevertheless, give yourself full credit for a spade return if you never want to play with your present partner again. Because that is exactly what is going to happen.

KEY LESSON POINTERS

1. WHEN PARTNER HAS A CHOICE OF EQUAL CARDS TO USE WHEN KNOCKING OUT A STOPPER AT NOTRUMP, THE CARD HE LEADS SHOULD BE INTERPRETED AS SUIT PREFERENCE. HOW ELSE ARE YOU SUPPOSED TO KNOW WHICH SUIT TO RETURN IF AND WHEN YOU GET THE LEAD?

2. VS A SUIT CONTRACT, THE SECOND EQUAL CAN BETTER BE USED TO GIVE COUNT. FOR EXAMPLE, WITH AN EVEN NUMBER CONTINUE WITH THE QUEEN (KQJx); WITH AN ODD NUMBER CONTINUE WITH THE JACK (KQJ, KQJxx).

3. THIS METHOD CAN ALSO BE USED BY THIRD HAND. ASSUME PARTNER LEADS A SUIT IN WHICH YOU HAVE A KQJ COMBINATION. YOU PLAY THE JACK AND IT HOLDS. CONTINUE WITH THE QUEEN HOLDING AN EVEN NUMBER OF CARDS, AND WITH THE KING HOLDING AN ODD NUMBER. I CAN'T BELIEVE I AM GIVING AWAY SO MANY OF MY SECRETS.

(11) ACELESS DOUBLE

North-South vulnerable
Dealer North

North
♠ 3 2
♡ K 8 7 6 5
♢ K 10 9 5
♣ A 9

West (You)
♠ K J 5 4
♡ 2
♢ Q J 4
♣ K Q 10 6 2

North	East	South	West
Pass	Pass	1 ♡	Dbl.
4 ♡	All Pass		

Opening Lead: ♣ K

1. Dummy wins and partner plays the ♣ 8. What do you make of that card?
2. Declarer continues by playing the king and ace of hearts, partner playing the four and the jack, as you discard a club.
    What are the possible trump positions?
3. Declarer continues by playing ace, king and a diamond, partner discarding the ♣ 3 on the third diamond.
    What do you think is going on, and what do you play now?
    (You remain with your four spades and the ♣ Q 10 6.)

ACELESS DOUBLE (SOLUTION)

North
♠ 3 2
♡ K 8 7 6 5
♢ K10 9 5
♣ A 9

West
♠ K J 5 4
♡ 2
♢ Q J 4
♣ K Q 10 6 2

East
♠ 10 9 8 7
♡ Q J 4
♢ 7 2
♣ J 8 4 3

South
♠ A Q 6
♡ A10 9 3
♢ A 8 6 3
♣ 7 5

1. Partner either has a doubleton, or an equal honor, in this case, the ♣ J. Time will tell.
2. Partner is either out of hearts or remains with the ♡ Q. Many players who do not open with a four card major in first or second seat will open with a four card major in third or fourth position.
3. A low club. The position should be clear. Declarer is known to have started with four diamonds, and partner must be showing the ♣ J with his high-low. If partner had a doubleton club, declarer's distribution would be either 1-4-4-4 or 0-5-4-4. In either case partner would still be bidding spades.

    Once you know that partner has the ♣ J, it must be 100% safe to lead a low club so that partner, rather than you, can break spades.

    Once again your defensive genius has defeated a contract. Of course, if declarer had ducked the opening lead, even a genius like you could not have defeated this contract. (You would be thrown in with a diamond after declarer had stripped the clubs and cashed the two top hearts.)

KEY LESSON POINTERS

1. WHEN YOU LEAD A HIGH HONOR AND PARTNER GIVES YOU AN ENCOURAGING SIGNAL HE EITHER HAS A DOUBLETON OR AN EQUAL HONOR. IF PARTNER HAS SUPPORTED THE SUIT, ASSUME AN EQUAL HONOR SIGNAL. OTHERWISE YOU MUST WORK IT OUT FROM THE BIDDING AND PLAY. MANY TIMES YOU WILL BE ABLE TO TELL PARTNER DOES NOT HAVE A DOUBLETON BECAUSE THAT WOULD GIVE DECLARER TOO MANY CARDS IN THE SUIT AND IT WOULD BE INCONSISTENT WITH THE BIDDING.
2. ONE ADVANTAGE OF LEADING THE ACE FROM ACE-KING IS THAT THIRD HAND CAN SIGNAL WITH THE JACK WHEN THE KING IS LED. HOWEVER, WHEN THE ACE IS IN THE DUMMY, IT DOESN'T MATTER WHICH METHOD YOU USE, BECAUSE THIRD HAND KNOWS THAT THE OPENING LEADER HAS THE KQ. PROBLEMS ARISE FOR THIRD HAND AS TO WHETHER TO SIGNAL WITH THE JACK WHEN THE KING IS LED FROM BOTH AK AND KQ WHEN THE ACE IS NOT IN THE DUMMY.

(12) THOSE WHO DOUBLE...

North-South vulnerable
Dealer East

North
♠ A K 9 7 5 4
♡ 3
◇ A
♣ Q 10 6 5 4

East (you)
♠ Q J 10 8
♡ 8
◇ K 4 3 2
♣ K J 9 8

East	South	West	North
Pass	1 ◇	3 ♡	3 ♠
Pass	3 NT	Pass	Pass
Dbl.	All Pass		

Opening Lead: ♡ K

Declarer wins the ♡ A and immediately plays ace, king and a spade, discarding two hearts from his hand. Partner also discards a heart on the third spade.

Where do you go from here?

THOSE WHO DOUBLE.... (SOLUTION)

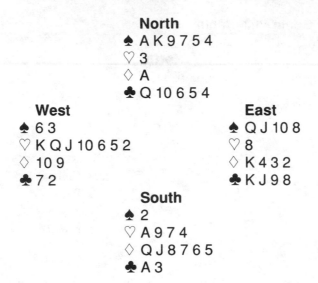

North
♠ A K 9 7 5 4
♡ 3
◇ A
♣ Q 10 6 5 4

West
♠ 6 3
♡ K Q J 10 6 5 2
◇ 10 9
♣ 7 2

East
♠ Q J 10 8
♡ 8
◇ K 4 3 2
♣ K J 9 8

South
♠ 2
♡ A 9 7 4
◇ Q J 8 7 6 5
♣ A 3

Careful! You must cash your winning spade and exit a diamond. You know that declarer started with one spade and four hearts. Furthermore you know that declarer must have all of the missing honors.

We can safely say that declarer either started with:

(a) ♠ x   ♡ Axxx   ◇ QJxxxx   ♣ Ax
(b) ♠ x   ♡ Axxx   ◇ QJxxx   ♣ Axx

First, let's see what develops if you do as suggested. Declarer will cash his two remaining spades (you discard diamonds), and with (a) will cross to the ♣ A and exit a diamond to your king. Fine. You win and lead a low club to dummy's ten, but take the last two club tricks with the king and jack.

He may play the same way with (b) or he may allow you to hold the ♣ 8 when he comes off dummy. You exit with a club and you still must make two more tricks. Play it out.

Now let's see what happens if you exit a diamond upon winning the first spade. Declarer will put you back in with a spade, discarding his last heart. You will be forced to lead a club to dummy's ten. After cashing dummy's two spade winners, declarer will cross to the ♣ A and play a diamond to your king. You can take no more than your ♣ K.

KEY LESSON POINTERS

1. SOME HANDS ARE HARDER TO DEFEND THAN OTHERS. THIS ONE FALLS INTO THE VERY HARD CATEGORY .
2. NON-VULNERABLE PREEMPTIVE JUMP OVERCALLS AT THE THREE LEVEL SOMETIMES CONTAIN SIX CARD SUITS. THIS ONE HAD SEVEN.
3. ON A HAND LIKE THIS, YOU CAN'T EXPECT ANY HELP FROM PARTNER. YOU ARE GOING TO HAVE TO TAKE FIVE TRICKS IN YOUR OWN HAND. THIS REQUIRES A LITTLE PLANNING TO SEE JUST WHAT WILL DEVELOP.
4. SOMETIMES THE BIDDING HAS BEEN SO REVEALING, AS HERE, THAT DECLARER KNOWS PRACTICALLY EVERY CARD IN YOUR HAND AND VICE VERSA. THIS TIME YOU TRIUMPH IF YOU AVOID GETTING YOURSELF ENDPLAYED TWICE!

(13) IN THE KNOW (1) (2) (3)

Neither side vulnerable
Dealer South

North
♠ Q 10
♡ 4 3 2
◇ A J 10 9 8 2
♣ 10 2

East (you)
♠ 9 7 6 5
♡ K Q J
◇ Q 5 4
♣ 9 8 3

South	West	North	East
1 ♣	Pass	1 ◇	Pass
2 ♡	Pass	3 ◇	Pass
3 NT	All Pass		

Opening Lead: ♠ 3

1. Dummy plays the ♠ 10. Which spade do you play?
    You play the ♠ 7, second high from four to give count.
2. Declarer wins the ♠ K and leads the ◇ 3 to the ◇ J,
    West playing the ◇ 7. Do you take this trick? If so, what do
    you return? If not, why not?
    You should duck the trick. There is a strong possibility
    that declarer has a doubleton diamond. If so, you can kill the
    suit by ducking the diamond – if the ♠ Q is not an entry to
    the dummy.
3. After you duck, declarer continues with the ◇ A, on
    which he plays the ◇ K, and a third diamond upon which he
    discards the ♠ A, partner discarding the ♠ 2.
    What is declarer's distribution?
    2-4-2-5.
4   You shift to the ♡ K which holds, partner playing the
    ♡ 5 .
    What do you do now?

IN THE KNOW (SOLUTION)

North
♠ Q 10
♡ 4 3 2
◇ A J 10 9 8 2
♣10 2

West
♠ J 8 4 3 2
♡ 7 6 5
◇ 7 6
♣ K J 7

East
♠ 9 7 6 5
♡ K Q J
◇ Q 5 4
♣ 9 8 3

South
♠ A K
♡ A 10 9 8
◇ K 3
♣ A Q 6 5 4

4.   Time to shift to a club. Partner needs two club honors to defeat the contract and you may have to lead the suit twice.

Notice that if you continue hearts, declarer makes the contract. He wins the second heart and exits a third. You win and play a club which declarer ducks to partner's jack. Partner can neither play a spade (dummy is high) or a club (declarer's hand is high).

However, if you play a club earlier, partner can win and exit a heart. When you are thrown in with a third heart you can exit a club. This defense allows you to take two clubs, two hearts, and a diamond.

KEY LESSON POINTERS

1.   WHEN PARTNER LEADS LOW VS. NOTRUMP AND THE DUMMY PLAYS A CARD THAT YOU, THIRD HAND, CANNOT TOP, GIVE COUNT IF THE CARD PLAYED FROM DUMMY IS THE QUEEN OR LOWER, GIVE ATTITUDE IF IT IS THE ACE OR KING.

2.   THE DIAMOND COMBINATION ON THIS HAND IS VERY INTERESTING. DECLARER MUST HAVE EXACTLY TWO DIAMONDS. IF HE HAD Kxx, HE WOULD HAVE STARTED WITH THE KING. IF HE HAD xx, PARTNER SHOULD PLAY THE KING FROM Kx. THEREFORE, IT IS ALMOST CERTAIN THAT DECLARER HAS Kx. THEREFORE, IT IS QUITE LIKELY HE HAS NO DUMMY ENTRY TO THE DIAMONDS OUTSIDE OF THE SUIT ITSELF. THAT IS WHY YOU MUST DUCK THE TRICK.

3.   WHEN YOUR PARTNER NEEDS A CERTAIN HOLDING TO DEFEAT THE CONTRACT (HERE, TWO CLUB HONORS EXCLUDING THE QJ), PLAY FOR HIM TO HOLD THOSE CARDS AND DEFEND ACCORDINGLY. YOU MUST VISUALIZE THAT IF YOU DON'T LEAD CLUBS EARLY WHILE PARTNER STILL HAS HEART EXIT CARDS, HE WILL BE ENDPLAYED UPON WINNING HIS FIRST CLUB TRICK.

(14) NICE LEAD

East-West vulnerable
Dealer North

North
♠ 5 2
♡ A K J
◇ 4 3
♣ A J 10 9 8 7

West (you)
♠ K 9 3
♡ 10 5 2
◇ K 10 8 6 2
♣ Q 2

North	East	South	West
1 ♣	Pass	1 ♠	Pass
2 ♣	Pass	2 NT	Pass
3 NT	All Pass		

Opening Lead: ◇ 6

Partner plays the ◇ Q, declarer the ◇ 7. At trick two partner returns the ◇ 9, declarer plays the ◇ J and you win the trick. Now what?

NICE LEAD (SOLUTION)

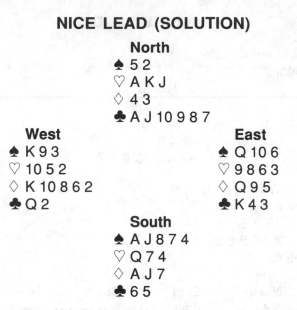

North
♠ 5 2
♡ A K J
♢ 4 3
♣ A J 10 9 8 7

West
♠ K 9 3
♡ 10 5 2
♢ K 10 8 6 2
♣ Q 2

East
♠ Q 10 6
♡ 9 8 6 3
♢ Q 9 5
♣ K 4 3

South
♠ A J 8 7 4
♡ Q 7 4
♢ A J 7
♣ 6 5

Did you return a high diamond to drive out the ace, waiting to get in with your ♠ K to run your diamonds? Nice play. Declarer made an overtrick because you forgot to count HIS TRICKS!

In order for your side to have any chance to defeat this contract partner must have the ♣ K, so assume he has it. Even so, that gives declarer five club tricks, the ace of diamonds you know about, and, judging from dummy's hearts, at least three tricks in that suit.

In other words, once partner's ♣ K is driven out, you are not going to have time to cash your diamonds. When partner switches to a spade upon winning ♣ K, declarer will simply rise with the ♠ A and play on clubs. Curtains.

What you have to do is try to develop two spade tricks before partner's ♣ K is removed. You must switch to a low spade at trick three. You are hoping to find something like the Q10 or the QJ of spades in partner's hand. If he has that combination you will score five tricks before the declarer can score nine. Remember, you are involved in a race here. You don't have TIME to work on the diamonds.

KEY LESSON POINTERS

1. YOU MUST ALWAYS KEEP TRACK OF DECLARER'S TRICKS.
2. IF YOU CAN SEE THAT YOU AND YOUR PARTNER ARE ONLY GOING TO GET THE LEAD ONE MORE TIME, YOU MUST TRY AND DEVELOP SOME TRICKS IN A HURRY.
3. SETTING UP A LONG SUIT AND THEN NOT BEING ABLE TO USE IT IS NOT EXACTLY WHAT THE DEFENDERS ARE TRYING TO DO.
4. COUNT DECLARER'S POINTS AS THEY ARE REVEALED DURING THE BIDDING AND THE PLAY. HERE YOU KNOW THAT DECLARER STARTED WITH 5 POINTS IN DIA-MONDS AND SURELY 2 IN HEARTS. HIS BIDDING SHOWS ABOUT 11 OR 12 HIGH CARD POINTS AND YOU HAVE ALREADY CONSIGNED THE ♣ K TO YOUR PARTNER. THEREFORE, DECLARER HAS NO MORE THAN 4 OR 5 POINTS IN SPADES AND PART-NER MUST HAVE AT LEAST THE QUEEN OR THE QUEEN   JACK OF SPADES. YOU ARE SO BRILLIANT.

(15) STRANGENESS

East-West vulnerable
Dealer South

North
♠ 4 2
♡ K J 10 6 4
♢ 9 6 4
♣ 4 3 2

East (you)
♠ 9 8 7 6 3
♡ 8 7
♢ A Q 3
♣ Q J 10

South	West	North	East
2 NT	Pass	3 ◇*	Pass
3 ♡	Pass	3 NT	Pass
4 ♡	All Pass		

*Transfer

Opening Lead: ♠ Q   (You lead Q from AKQ)

Partner's ♠ Q holds, declarer playing the five, you the three. At trick two partner shifts to the ◇ 2 which you win with the ◇ A. Now what?

STRANGENESS (SOLUTION)

North
♠ 4 2
♡ K J 10 6 4
◇ 9 6 4
♣ 4 3 2

West	East
♠ Q J 10	♠ 9 8 7 6 3
♡ 5 3 2	♡ 8 7
◇ K 7 5 2	◇ A Q 3
♣ 9 6 5	♣ Q J 10

South
♠ A K 5
♡ A Q 9
◇ J 10 8
♣ A K 8 7

Return a low diamond. For openers, partner does not have the ♠ A K Q. That would leave declarer with 18 high card points and his opening 2NT bid showed 20-22.

Therefore, declarer has the ♠ A K and is planning a little something. What is that little devil up to? Well, he is almost surely planning to discard a club on his own winning spade and then ruff a club, setting up the suit for a diamond discard.

Your partner has worked all of this out and has made the winning shift to a diamond. Don't tell me, just don't tell me, you didn't return a diamond.

If nothing else, you should have known it couldn't be right to shift to a club when you are looking at QJ10. That's the tip off, never lead what it looks like you should. Just kidding. In this case you should be able to read declarer's intentions and thwart him by cashing your diamond winners before one of them goes bye-bye on a fourth club.

KEY LESSON POINTERS

1. WHEN A GOOD PLAYER MAKES A STRANGE LOOKING PLAY, IT'S UP TO YOU TO FIGURE OUT WHAT HE IS UP TO.

2. WHEN YOU HAVE WORKED OUT THAT DECLARER HAS AKx FACING xx AT A SUIT CONTRACT AND HAS DUCKED THE OPENING LEAD, THERE IS USUALLY ONLY ONE ANSWER. HE IS TRYING TO SET UP ANOTHER SUIT BEFORE YOU CAN CASH SOME QUICK WINNERS IN HIS WEAK SUIT. THIS IS A VERY CLEVER PLOY AND IT TOOK DEFENDERS AS ALERT AS BOTH YOU AND YOUR PARTNER TO FOIL IT. YOU DID FOIL IT, DIDN'T YOU?

3. 99 TIMES OUT OF ONE HUNDRED WHEN PARTNER LEADS THE QUEEN AND NEITHER THE ACE NOR THE KING IS VISIBLE, AND THE QUEEN HOLDS, PARTNER WILL HAVE BEEN LEADING FROM AKQ COMBINATION. THIS HAND IS THE ONE OUT OF ONE HUNDRED.

(16) THERE MUST BE A WAY

East-West vulnerable
Dealer East

North
♠ J 3 2
♡ 4 2
♢ A K J 8 7 6 5
♣ 4

West (you)
♠ A 10 7 4
♡ A 6
♢ Q 10 9
♣ J 10 9 5

East	South	West	North
Pass	1 ♡	Pass	2 ♢
Pass	3 ♡	Pass	4 ♡
All Pass			

Opening Lead: ♣ J

East plays the ♣ 8 and declarer wins the ♣ A and ruffs the ♣ 6 in dummy, partner playing the ♣ 2. At trick three declarer leads a trump to his king and your ace.
1. How do you read the club position?
2. What do you play now?

THERE MUST BE A WAY (SOLUTION)

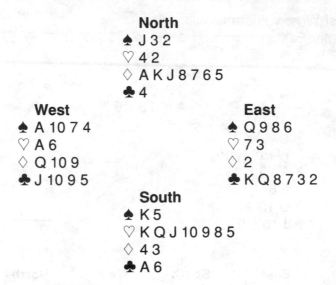

North
♠ J 3 2
♡ 4 2
◇ A K J 8 7 6 5
♣ 4

West
♠ A 10 7 4
♡ A 6
◇ Q 10 9
♣ J 10 9 5

East
♠ Q 9 8 6
♡ 7 3
◇ 2
♣ K Q 8 7 3 2

South
♠ K 5
♡ K Q J 10 9 8 5
◇ 4 3
♣ A 6

1.　Partner should have started with six clubs, indicating declarer is now void. Partner's ♣ 8 was an attitude card, his ♣ 2 was a present count card.

　　When giving present count, the signaller plays a low card to indicate an odd number of cards at the time of the signal, and a higher card to indicate an even number. When East played the second club he had KQ732 remaining and played his lowest card to show an odd number. If his original club holding had been something like KQ875, he would play 8 then 7.

2.　A diamond . If declarer needed to take any diamond discards (or was void in diamonds) he could have done so earlier. Given the club position (declarer probably has a doubleton), there is a good chance that declarer has a doubleton diamond and partner a singleton. If you switch to a diamond, declarer will not be able to get off dummy without allowing you to give partner a ◇ ruff.

KEY LESSON POINTERS

1. WHEN PARTNER LEADS AN HONOR, THIRD HAND SIGNALS ATTITUDE. IF THIRD HAND HAS SHOWN SIX OR MORE CARDS IN THE SUIT, THIRD HAND'S FIRST PLAY IS SUIT PREFERENCE.

2. WHEN DECLARER DOES NOT TAKE IMMEDIATE DISCARDS ON A LONG, STRONG SUIT ON THE TABLE, THE DEFENDERS MUST ASSUME THAT THERE IS NO URGENCY TO TAKE THOSE DISCARDS AND PLAN ACCORDINGLY.

3. WHEN DECLARER APPEARS TO HAVE A VERY MINIMUM HIGH CARD COUNT FOR A JUMP REBID, ASSUME A SEVEN CARD SUIT TO MAKE UP THE SLACK.

(17) DOUBLE FIT

Neither side vulnerable
Dealer South

North
♠ 2
♡ Q J 8 6
◇ A 4 3 2
♣ J 6 4 3

East (you)
♠ Q 5 4 3
♡ 5 4
◇ K Q 10 8
♣ K 10 8

South	West	North	East
1 ♡	2 ♡*	4 ♡	4 ♠
5 ♡	All Pass		

*Spades and a minor - at least 5-5.

Opening Lead: ♠ 7

Declarer wins the ♠ A and leads the ♠ 9. Partner plays the ♠ 10 and dummy ruffs low.

At trick three, declarer leads a low club. Which club do you play? Why?

DOUBLE FIT (SOLUTION)

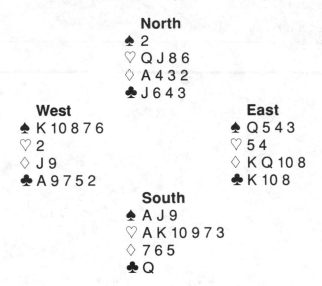

North
♠ 2
♡ Q J 8 6
♢ A 4 3 2
♣ J 6 4 3

West
♠ K 10 8 7 6
♡ 2
♢ J 9
♣ A 9 7 5 2

East
♠ Q 5 4 3
♡ 5 4
♢ K Q 10 8
♣ K 10 8

South
♠ A J 9
♡ A K 10 9 7 3
♢ 7 6 5
♣ Q

The ♣ K. Partner's second suit must be clubs. Declarer is known to have a singleton. If that singleton is the queen and you play low, declarer will be able to ruff out your ♣ K for a diamond discard. That would put one of your diamond winners to sleep. For shame.

KEY LESSON POINTERS

1. AFTER YOU PLAY THIRD HAND HIGH, YOUR SECOND PLAY IN THE SUIT IS PRESENT COUNT. WITH THREE OR FIVE CARDS REMAINING IN THE SUIT, PLAY LOW; WITH TWO CARDS REMAINING PLAY YOUR HIGHER ONE; WITH FOUR CARDS REMAINING, PLAY THE HIGHEST ONE YOU CAN AFFORD.
   AFTER HAVING PLAYED THE ♠ QUEEN TO THE FIRST TRICK, PLAY THE UNDERLINED SPADE THE SECOND TIME THE SUIT IS LED: Q8̲3 Q54̲3 Q8̲763 Q96543̲.

2. WHENEVER PARTNER SHOWS A TWO-SUITER, THE SECOND SUIT UNKNOWN, YOU CAN USUALLY TELL WHICH SUIT THAT IS WHEN THE DUMMY COMES DOWN. IN THIS CASE, IT IS MORE LIKELY TO BE CLUBS THAN DIAMONDS. BESIDES, IF PARTNER'S SECOND SUIT WERE DIAMONDS, DECLARER WOULD HAVE A FISTFUL OF CLUBS AND WOULD BE DRAWING TRUMPS FIRST.

3. THERE ARE TIMES WHEN SECOND HAND HIGH IS NECESSARY. GIVEN THIS CLUB POSITION, A POSITION WHICH YOU SUSPECT, YOU SHOULD RISE WITH THE ♣ K. IF IT WORKS, FIND SOMEONE WHO WRITES A NEWSPAPER COLUMN AND TELL HIM ABOUT IT. IF IT DOESN'T, YOUR PARTNER WILL FIND EVERYBODY ELSE AND TELL THEM ABOUT IT.

(18) NO RESPECT (1) (2)

North-South vulnerable
Dealer North

North
♠ K Q 7 6
♡ A 8
◇ A K 7 5
♣ J 5 4

West (you)
♠ A J 10 4
♡ 9 7 6
◇ Q J 9 2
♣ 9 2

North	East	South	West
1 NT	3 ♡	4 ♣	Pass
4 ♡	Dbl.	Rdbl.	Pass
6 ♣	All Pass		

Opening Lead: ♡ 6

Dummy wins the ♡ A, as declarer produces the ♡ Q. A trump goes to the king in the closed hand and a low spade is led.
1.   Which spade do you play?
     You play low. Dummy's queen wins, and partner plays the ♠ 9.
2.   Declarer returns to his hand via a second trump, partner follows, and another spade is led.
     What are declarer's possible distributions, and which spade do you play this time?
     Declarer should be either 3-1-3-6 or 4-1-2-6, and you should play low again!
3.   You do play low and dummy's king wins, partner contributing the ♠ 8. When declarer plays a third spade from dummy, partner discards a heart and you win the trick.
     Now what?

NO RESPECT (SOLUTION)

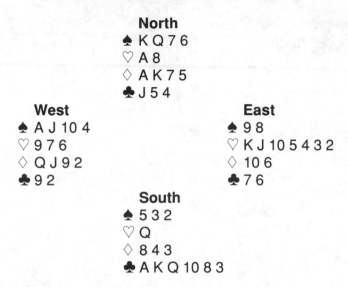

North
♠ K Q 7 6
♡ A 8
♢ A K 7 5
♣ J 5 4

West
♠ A J 10 4
♡ 9 7 6
♢ Q J 9 2
♣ 9 2

East
♠ 9 8
♡ K J 10 5 4 3 2
♢ 10 6
♣ 7 6

South
♠ 5 3 2
♡ Q
♢ 8 4 3
♣ A K Q 10 8 3

Play a fourth spade and kill dummy's spade threat against you. You know declarer's distribution at this point, and if you don't play a fourth spade, the run of the clubs will squeeze you between spades and diamonds.

KEY LESSON POINTERS

1. A REDOUBLE OF A DOUBLED CUE BID USUALLY SHOWS SECOND ROUND CONTROL IN THE SUIT: EITHER A SINGLETON OR THE KING.
2. LEAD LOW FROM THREE SMALL IN PARTNER'S SUIT IF YOU HAVE NOT SUPPORTED THE SUIT. IF YOU HAVE, LEAD HIGH.
3. DEFENDERS MUST MAKE AN EFFORT TO COUNT EVERY HAND. HERE THE COUNT IS VITAL. KNOWING DECLARER'S DISTRIBUTION AFTER PARTNER FOLLOWS TO THE SECOND SPADE GIVES YOU THE OPPORTUNITY TO GET YOURSELF OFF A SQUEEZE. HAD YOU WON AN EARLIER SPADE YOU WOULD HAVE BEEN POWER-LESS TO AVOID THE SQUEEZE.
4. YES, DECLARER COULD HAVE SQUEEZED YOU ANYWAY HAD HE LED A HEART FROM DUMMY AND DISCARDED HIS LAST SPADE. INSTEAD OF LEADING THE SUIT HIMSELF A THIRD TIME. LATER HE COULD RUFF A SPADE AND THEN RUN HIS CLUBS AND SQUEEZE YOU. FORTUNATELY, MOST DECLARERS ARE NOT THAT CLEVER, UNLESS THEY HAVE READ MY BOOKS.

(19) UP TO YOU

East-West vulnerable
Dealer North

North
♠ K 4 3 2
♡ K 10 8 7
♢ A K 2
♣ K Q

West (you)
♠ Q 9 7
♡ J 9 4
♢ 8 7 6
♣ J 10 9 8

North	East	South	West
1 ♢	Pass	1 ♠	Pass
3 ♠	Pass	4 NT*	Pass
5 ♡**	Pass	6 ♠	All Pass

*Roman Key Card Blackwood
**Two Key Cards lacking the trump queen.

Opening Lead: ♣ J (partner plays the ♣ 2)

Declarer wins your opening lead in dummy, cashes the ♠ K and leads a spade to the ace, partner discarding a club.

Declarer continues with the ♣ A and three rounds of diamonds, partner playing high-low before exiting a spade to your queen, partner discarding yet another club.

1. What is declarer's exact distribution?
2. What do you play now?

UP TO YOU (SOLUTION)

North
♠ K 4 3 2
♡ K 10 8 7
♢ A K 2
♣ K Q

West
♠ Q 9 7
♡ J 9 4
♢ 8 7 6
♣ J 10 9 8

East
♠ 6
♡ Q 6 5
♢ 9 5 4 3
♣ 7 5 4 3 2

South
♠ A J 10 8 5
♡ A 3 2
♢ Q J 10
♣ A 6

1. 5-3-3-2
2. You should exit with the ♡ J. In fact, that is the only card in your hand that you can play at this point to defeat the contract!

    You should think like this: I know that declarer has three hearts headed by the ace (otherwise there is no problem). If I lead a low heart, declarer may play low from dummy forcing my partner's queen; I will now be subjected to a heart finesse. If I lead the ♡ 9, declarer will cover with the ♡ 10 and once again we will take zero heart tricks.

    However, if I lead the ♡ J, twist and turn as he will, declarer will have to concede a heart trick.

KEY LESSON POINTERS

1. KEEP COUNTING ON DEFENSE. THIS IS A RECORDING.
2. PARTNER'S PLAY OF THE ♣ 2 AT TRICK ONE SHOULD BE A COUNT, NOT AN ATTITUDE SIGNAL. IF HE HAD THE ♣ A HE WOULD HAVE TAKEN THE TRICK, SO HE IS KNOWN NOT TO HOLD THE ♣ A. THEREFORE, HE MIGHT AS WELL GIVE COUNT. THE GENERAL RULE IS: WHEN A DEFENDER CANNOT LOGICALLY HOLD A HIGH HONOR IN A SUIT PARTNER HAS LED, HE GIVES COUNT, NOT ATTITUDE.
3. THE HEART COMBINATION IS ONE YOU SHOULD KNOW. YOU WOULD ALSO PLAY AN HONOR IN THIS POSITION FROM ANY OF THESE HOLDINGS: Q9x, J9xx OR Q9xx.

(20) NOTHING FANCY

North-South vulnerable
Dealer North

North
♠ A Q 6
♡ 3 2
◊ Q 5 4
♣ J 10 6 4 3

West (you)
♠ 9 5 3
♡ A Q 8 6 5
◊ 10 9 8
♣ K 9

North	East	South	West
Pass	Pass	1 ♣	1 ♡
2 ♣	Pass	2 NT	Pass
3 NT	All Pass		

Opening Lead: ♡ 6

1. Partner plays the ♡ 10 which declarer wins with the
    ♡ J.
    What is the heart position?
2. Declarer crosses to the ◊ Q, partner playing the ◊ 7. The
    ♣ J is led to partner's ♣ 2, declarer's ♣ 5, and your ♣ K.
    What do you make of the club and diamond positions,
    and what do you lead now?

NOTHING FANCY (SOLUTION)

North
♠ A Q 6
♡ 3 2
◇ Q 5 4
♣ J 10 6 4 3

West
♠ 9 5 3
♡ A Q 8 6 5
◇ 10 9 8
♣ K 9

East
♠ K 8 4
♡ 10 7 4
◇ J 7 3 2
♣ 8 7 2

South
♠ J 10 7 2
♡ K J 9
◇ A K 6
♣ A Q 5

1. Declarer has the ♡ K J 9. You cannot tell whether he has three or four hearts.

2. In diamonds partner should have a four card suit as the ◇ 7 should be a count card.

    In clubs, partner has either a singleton or a three card holding, as the ♣ 2 should be a count card.

    Since there is a good chance that (1) the clubs are blocked, and (2) your partner holds the ♠ K, you should shift to a spade before declarer can unblock his club suit.

KEY LESSON POINTERS

1. ACCURATE DEFENDERS ALWAYS TAKE A READING IN THE SUIT THEY HAVE LED, USING PARTNER'S PLAY IN THIRD CHAIR TO GUIDE THEM. IN THIS CASE, THE PLAY OF THE ♡ 10 HAS DENIED BOTH THE NINE AND THE KING.

2. IN GENERAL, PARTNER WILL GIVE YOU COUNT IN ANY SUIT DECLARER ATTACKS, PARTICULARLY WHEN HE IS THE WEAKER OF THE TWO HANDS. (THE STRONG HAND DOES NOT ALWAYS GIVE AN HONEST COUNT.)

3. WHEN GIVING STANDARD COUNT, PLAY LOW-HIGH WITH AN ORIGINAL HOLDING OF AN ODD NUMBER OF CARDS, HIGH-LOW WITH AN EVEN NUMBER OF CARDS.

4. MANY PAIRS NOW GIVE UPSIDE DOWN COUNT SIGNALS. THEY SIMPLY REVERSE THE PROCEDURE. LOW-HIGH SHOWS AN EVEN NUMBER OF CARDS, HIGH-LOW AN ODD NUMBER.

5. COUNT DECLARER'S POINTS AS THEY ARE REVEALED FROM THE PLAY. HERE DECLARER HAS SHOWN FOUR POINTS IN HEARTS, SEVEN POINTS IN DIAMONDS AND PROBABLY SIX IN CLUBS. IF THIS IS ALL TRUE, HE CAN HARDLY HAVE THE ♠ K AS WELL, OR ELSE HE WOULD HAVE OPENED 2NT WITH HIS 20 COUNT. MOST PLAYERS OPEN 2NT WITH 20-22 POINTS THESE DAYS. WITH 23-24 THEY OPEN 2 ♣ AND REBID 2NT.

(21) NAILED (1)

Neither side vulnerable
Dealer West

North
♠ 9 8 4
♡ K Q J 9 7
♢ A J 10 6
♣ 8

East (you)
♠ J 2
♡ A 10 6 5
♢ 8 7 2
♣ A 6 3 2

West	North	East	South
2 ♠*	Pass	Pass	3 ♣
Pass	3 ♡	Pass	3 NT
All Pass			

*Weak

Opening Lead: ♠ Q

1. Which spade do you play at trick one?
   You unblock the ♠ J and partner continues with the
   ♠ 10 which drives out declarer's ♠ A.
2. At trick three declarer leads the ♣ K and partner plays
   the ♣ 10. How do you plan the defense?

NAILED (SOLUTION)

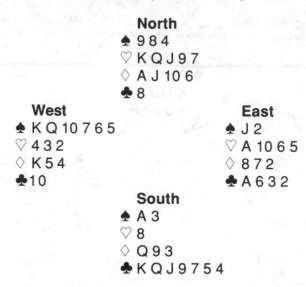

North
♠ 9 8 4
♡ K Q J 9 7
♢ A J 10 6
♣ 8

West
♠ K Q 10 7 6 5
♡ 4 3 2
♢ K 5 4
♣ 10

East
♠ J 2
♡ A 10 6 5
♢ 8 7 2
♣ A 6 3 2

South
♠ A 3
♡ 8
♢ Q 9 3
♣ K Q J 9 7 5 4

Declarer appears to have solid clubs missing the ace and if he has the ♢ K as well there is no defense. Therefore, you must assume partner has the ♢ K.

You should win the ♣ A and play the ♡ A and the ♡ 10 freezing declarer in dummy. The best declarer can do is run his good hearts reducing to four diamonds and a spade. West saves three good spades and king doubleton of diamonds.

If declarer is smart enough to exit from dummy with a spade, he goes down two tricks, otherwise three.

KEY LESSON POINTERS

1. THE LEAD OF THE QUEEN FROM A KQ10 COMBINATION AT NOTRUMP HAS BE-
   COME CONVENTIONAL. IT REQUESTS PARTNER TO PLAY THE JACK IF HE HAS
   IT. LACKING THE JACK, THIRD HAND PLAYS LOW UNLESS HE HAS THE ACE, IN
   WHICH CASE HE EITHER OVERTAKES OR SIGNALS.

2. WHEN PARTNER NEEDS A SPECIFIC CARD TO DEFEAT THE CONTRACT (HERE
   THE DIAMOND KING), PLAY HIM FOR IT.

3. VISUALIZING DECLARER'S INABILITY TO GET TO HIS HAND AND LOCKING HIM
   IN DUMMY IS AN EXPERT DEFENSIVE PLAY. NOTICE THE CONTINUATION OF
   THE ♡ 10 RATHER THAN A LOW HEART. IF YOU RETAIN THE HEART TEN,
   THEN YOU WILL BE THROWN IN WITH IT AND FORCED TO LEAD A MINOR SUIT.
   ONCE YOU LEAD A MINOR SUIT, DECLARER LOSES NO MORE TRICKS. IF YOU
   EVEN THOUGHT OF DOING THIS, I'M IMPRESSED.

(22) GOOD HAND ON THE BIDDING

Neither side vulnerable
Dealer South

North
♠ A 7
♡ J 6 5
◇ Q 10 8 4
♣ A Q J 4

East (you)
♠ K 5 3
♡ K Q 7 4
◇ 6 3
♣ K 9 8 7

South	West	North	East
1 ◇	Pass	2 ♣	Pass
2 ♠	Pass	4 ◇	Pass
4 ♡	Pass	4 ♠	Pass
4 NT	Pass	5 ♡	Dbl.
5 NT	Pass	6 ♣	Pass
6 ◇	All Pass		

Opening Lead: ♡ 2

Dummy plays low, you play the ♡ Q, and declarer wins. At trick two declarer leads the ♣ 2 to the ♣ A and continues with the ♣ Q.
1. Is your play determined by the club partner has played at trick two?
2. Assume your partner has played (a) the ♣ 3, (b) the ♣ 6, what would you do in each case?

GOOD HAND ON THE BIDDING (SOLUTION)

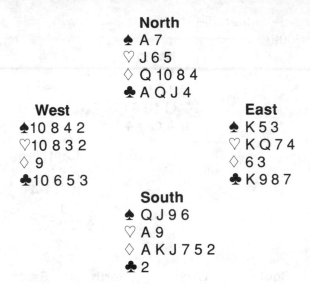

North
♠ A 7
♡ J 6 5
◇ Q 10 8 4
♣ A Q J 4

West
♠ 10 8 4 2
♡ 10 8 3 2
◇ 9
♣ 10 6 5 3

East
♠ K 5 3
♡ K Q 7 4
◇ 6 3
♣ K 9 8 7

South
♠ Q J 9 6
♡ A 9
◇ A K J 7 5 2
♣ 2

1-2. It shouldn't be. Declarer must have a singleton club, or else why didn't he finesse the club? Is he giving up a club trick with a known heart loser?

You should duck this trick quickly, regardless of the club your partner plays.

If declarer misplays the hand he will go down. He will ruff the ♣ Q; enter dummy with a trump and ruff a low club hoping to drop the ♣ K. When that doesn't happen he will be obliged to take the spade finesse and will go down, down, down.

If you cover the club, not only will the declarer make the slam but he will probably treat you like a long lost relative for the rest of your life.

KEY LESSON POINTERS

1. WHEN DECLARER HAS AN AQJ COMBINATION IN THE DUMMY AND LEADS LOW TO THE ACE FOLLOWED BY THE QUEEN, CHANCES ARE OVERWHELMING THAT HE HAS A SINGLETON.

2. ALTHOUGH PARTNER WILL USUALLY GIVE COUNT IN THE OFF SUITS, SOME PLAYERS ARE RELUCTANT TO DO SO VS. STRONG OPPOSITION FOR FEAR THAT IT MAY GIVE AWAY TOO MUCH INFORMATION. AGAINST SLAMS, YOU HAVE TO BE CAREFUL ABOUT GIVING A GOOD DECLARER TOO MUCH INFORMATION.

3. SOMETIMES YOU WILL BE FACED WITH THE AWFUL DECISION OF WHETHER TO BELIEVE PARTNER'S COUNT CARD OR THE LOGIC OF THE LINE OF PLAY THAT DECLARER HAS ADOPTED. UNLESS YOU ARE PLAYING WITH A RELIGIOUS COUNT GIVER, BELIEVE THE LINE OF PLAY DECLARER HAS ADOPTED – UNLESS DECLARER IS TOTALLY INCOMPETENT OR ONE OF YOUR EX-PARTNERS.

(23) HAH! (1)

Neither side vulnerable
Dealer South

North
♠ 7 5
♡ K J 10 6
♢ Q 5 2
♣ A 9 7 6

West (you)
♠ K Q 10 3 2
♡ 3 2
♢ 6 4
♣ K J 8 2

South	West	North	East
1 ♡	1 ♠	3 ♡	3 ♠
4 ♡	All Pass		

Opening Lead: ♠ K

Partner plays the ♠ 9 and your ♠ K holds. You try a low spade at trick two and partner wins the ♠ A, declarer playing the ♠ J.

At trick three partner switches to the ♢ 10, declarer winning the ace.

1.   At trick four declarer leads the ♣ 3 toward dummy. Which club do you play?

You play low and dummy wins the ♣ A, partner playing the ♣ 5.

2.   Declarer continues by playing the ♡ K and the ♡ J to the ♡ A, partner playing up the line. Next comes the ♢ J and the ♢ K from declarer's hand, partner playing the ♢ 9 and the ♢ 3.

Declarer now leads the ♣ 10 from his hand. Which club do you play?

HAH! (SOLUTION)

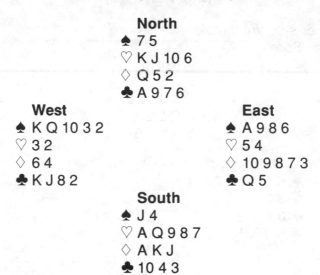

North
♠ 7 5
♡ K J 10 6
♦ Q 5 2
♣ A 9 7 6

West
♠ K Q 10 3 2
♡ 3 2
♦ 6 4
♣ K J 8 2

East
♠ A 9 8 6
♡ 5 4
♦ 10 9 8 7 3
♣ Q 5

South
♠ J 4
♡ A Q 9 8 7
♦ A K J
♣ 10 4 3

What an insult! South doesn't think you can play a lick. You should rise with the ♣ K, your partner's ♣ Q is sure to fall, and then you can cash the ♣ J for the setting trick.

How can you know to do this? First of all, you have a complete count on the South hand. Partner has shown five diamonds by playing a high diamond (present count) on the second lead of the suit.

Failing that, you can still tell that declarer had only three diamonds by the way he is playing the suit.

Once you have determined that South started with three clubs, you should realize that partner has the ♣ Q. Why? Because if declarer had ♣ Q 10x he wouldn't play the hand like this. He would strip the hand without cashing the ♣ A and simply lead a club to the nine and claim.

Notice that if you do not play the ♣ K, partner will be endplayed upon winning the ♣ Q and will have to surrender a ruff and a sluff allowing declarer to make an unmakeable game.

KEY LESSON POINTERS

1. MOST SPARKLING DEFENSIVE PLAYS COME FROM COUNTING THE HAND.
2. GIVE DECLARER CREDIT FOR NOT PLAYING THE HAND IN A LOONY-TUNE FASHION – UNLESS YOU'VE SEEN HIM PLAY BEFORE.
3. WHEN YOU GET DOWN TO A ONE SUIT POSITION AND YOU HAVE A COUNT ON THE HAND, YOU MUST INFER BY THE WAY DECLARER IS PLAYING THE HAND WHAT HE HAS IN THE CRITICAL SUIT.
4. AS A GENERAL RULE DO NOT SPLIT YOUR HONORS EARLY IN THE HAND WHEN DECLARER LEADS UP TO A BROKEN HOLDING IN DUMMY. FOR EXAMPLE, HAD YOU PLAYED THE ♣ J AT TRICK FOUR, YOU WOULD HAVE RUINED THE DEFENSE. AFTER DUMMY WINS THE ♣ A, CLUBS REALLY ARE BLOCKED AND YOU CAN NO LONGER DEFEAT THE CONTRACT IF DECLARER STRIPS THE HAND BEFORE PLAYING A SECOND CLUB.
5. IF YOU WERE EVEN THINKING THAT YOUR PARTNER MIGHT HOLD THE ♡ Q, FORGET IT. FIRST, MOST PLAYERS PLAY FIVE CARD MAJORS THESE DAYS. SECOND, IF DECLARER HAD AN EIGHT CARD HEART FIT HE WOULD HAVE TAKEN THE FINESSE IN HEARTS ONE WAY OR THE OTHER.

(24) GOOD DEFENSE (1) (2) (3)

Both sides vulnerable
Dealer North

North
♠ A 10 2
♡ A J 10 3
◊ 10 4
♣ K J 10 6

East (you)
♠ J 8 7 6
♡ 9 6 2
◊ Q J 7
♣ A 9 8

North	East	South	West
1 ♣	Pass	1 ♠	Pass
2 ♠	Pass	3 ♠	Pass
4 ♠	All Pass		

Opening Lead: ◊ K (K from AK)

1.   Which diamond do you play at trick one?
     You play the ◊ Q, promising the ◊ J, and partner contin-
ues with the ◊ 2 to your ◊ J.
2.   What is the diamond position, and what do you return at
trick three? Why?
     Partner apparently has four diamonds headed by the AK,
and you should return a third diamond, forcing dummy to
ruff and enhancing your trump trick.
3.   You play a third diamond, declarer plays low and
partner's ◊ 8 is ruffed low in dummy. Declarer continues
with the ♠ A, all following low and the ♠ 10. Do you
cover?
     Only if declarer is a close relative.
4.   You play low and declarer wins the ♠ K, partner
discarding a low heart. Declarer continues with the ♡ K and
then ♡ Q overtaking with the ♡ A. He then plays the ♡ J,
discarding the ◊ 9, and leads the ♡ 10. What was
declarer's original distribution, and what do you play now?

GOOD DEFENSE (SOLUTION)

North
♠ A 10 2
♡ A J 10 3
♢ 10 4
♣ K J 10 6

West
♠ 5
♡ 8 7 5 4
♢ A K 8 2
♣ Q 5 4 2

East
♠ J 8 7 6
♡ 9 6 2
♢ Q J 7
♣ A 9 8

South
♠ K Q 9 4 3
♡ K Q
♢ 9 6 5 3
♣ 7 3

4.   Declarer is known to be 5-2-4-2.

You should discard a club on the fourth heart. Although declarer can still make the hand if he ruffs his good heart and leads a club to the jack, you don't have to help him along.

If declarer discards a club on the fourth heart, he can no longer make the hand. You will always come to a club and a spade.

If you ruff, declarer will overruff, draw your last trump and then have to guess the club position. True, he may still go down, but you have a much better chance of defeating the contract by not ruffing. As long as you know declarer's entire hand, you should be able to see that if declarer fails to ruff his own good heart, he will have no further chance.

KEY LESSON POINTERS

1. DROPPING THE QUEEN UNDER PARTNER'S LEAD OF THE KING (OR THE ACE IF THE ACE IS FROM ACE-KING) PROMISES THE JACK. THE ONLY TIMES THAT IT DOES NOT ARE WHEN THE QUEEN IS SINGLETON OR THE JACK IS IN DUMMY. WHEN THE JACK IS IN DUMMY, IT IS PERMISSIBLE TO PLAY THE QUEEN FROM QUEEN-DOUBLETON..

2. WHEN PARTNER RETURNS THE ♢ 2 AT TRICK TWO HE INDICATES AN ORIGINAL HOLDING OF FOUR DIAMONDS. WITH MORE THAN FOUR DIAMONDS, HE SHOULD RETURN HIS ORIGINAL FOURTH BEST DIAMOND. FOR EXAMPLE, WITH ♢ A K 8 6 3, HE SHOULD RETURN THE SIX.

3. AN EVEN BETTER WAY IS TO RETURN THE LOWEST CARD FROM AN ORIGINAL HOLDING OF FOUR OR SIX CARDS, PARTNER USING THE BIDDING TO WORK OUT WHICH IT IS. WITH AN ORIGINAL HOLDING OF FIVE CARDS, RETURN THE HIGHEST SPOT CARD YOU CAN AFFORD. THUS, FROM AK8642, RETURN THE DEUCE. FROM AK862 RETURN THE EIGHT.

(25) ON YOUR SHOULDERS

Neither side vulnerable
Dealer South

　　　　　　　　North
　　　　　　　　♠ J 10 7
　　　　　　　　♡ 3 2
　　　　　　　　◇ A K
　　　　　　　　♣ K Q 7 5 3 2

West (you)
♠ 8 4 3 2
♡ A 6 4
◇ J 10 9 7 6
♣ 4

South	West	North	East
1 ♠	Pass	2 ♣	Pass
3 ♡	Pass	3 ♣	Pass
4 ♣	Pass	4 ◇	Pass
4 NT	Pass	5 ◇	Pass
6 ♠	All Pass		

　　　　Opening Lead:　◇ J

　　Declarer wins the ◇ A, crosses to the ♠ A, cashes the ♣ A, and leads a spade to the jack, partner discarding a low diamond. Next declarer plays two more rounds of spades, partner discarding two more diamonds, and dummy discarding a club. Declarer leads a club to dummy as you shed a diamond and leads a heart to his jack, partner playing the ♡ 5.

　　At the time dummy leads a heart, dummy has two hearts, the blank ◇ K, and the ♣ Q 7 5. You have three hearts and three diamonds.

　　1. What is declarer's distribution?
　　2. Do you win this trick? If so, what do you return?

ON YOUR SHOULDERS (SOLUTION)

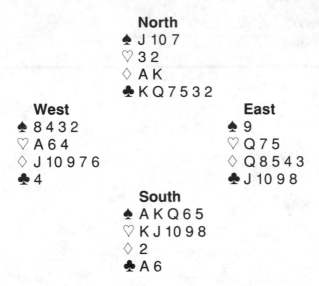

North
♠ J 10 7
♡ 3 2
◇ A K
♣ K Q 7 5 3 2

West
♠ 8 4 3 2
♡ A 6 4
◇ J 10 9 7 6
♣ 4

East
♠ 9
♡ Q 7 5
◇ Q 8 5 4 3
♣ J 10 9 8

South
♠ A K Q 6 5
♡ K J 10 9 8
◇ 2
♣ A 6

1.   5-5-1-2. What else could it possibly be, given the way the play is going? If declarer had a second diamond he could set up the club easily enough. If declarer had a third club, he would have 13 tricks off the top without a heart lead.

2.   You should duck the ♡ J. Declarer will have to lead hearts from his own hand as he has no more entries to dummy. If partner has the likely ♡ Q you defeat the contract by ducking.

   If you take the trick you will either have to return a heart, gobbling up partner's queen, or lead a minor suit card giving declarer a much-needed dummy entry to repeat the heart finesse.

KEY LESSON POINTERS

1. KEEP COUNTING AS THE PLAY DEVELOPS. THIS IS A RECORDING.

2. ALONG WITH COUNTING, WHICH AT TIMES CANNOT BE 100% SURE, YOU MUST USE A LITTLE COMMON SENSE. FOR EXAMPLE, WHY ISN'T DECLARER SETTING UP THE CLUBS? ANSWER: NO DUMMY ENTRY TO USE THEM ONCE THEY ARE ESTABLISHED.

3. IN GENERAL, YOU SHOULD NOT LEAD SINGLETONS VS. SLAMS WHEN YOU HOLD AN OUTSIDE ACE. PARTNER CANNOT BE EXPECTED TO HOLD THE ACE OF THE SINGLETON SUIT, NOR THE ACE OF TRUMPS – THE REASON YOU NORMALLY LEAD SINGLETONS VS. VOLUNTARILY BID SLAMS. OF COURSE IF THE OPPONENTS ARE SACRIFICING, IT IS A DIFFERENT MATTER.

4. WHEN DECLARER WILL BE FORCED TO PLAY THE SECOND ROUND OF A SUIT FROM HIS OWN HAND, IT IS FREQUENTLY RIGHT TO DUCK THE FIRST ROUND, IN EFFECT ENDPLAYING THE DECLARER.

Section III
DEFENSE

(26) NO PROBLEM

Neither side vulnerable
Dealer West

North
♠ Q 7 6 5
♡ J 5 4
◇ K 10 9
♣ A 7 4

East (you)
♠ 4 3 2
♡ Q 9 3
◇ J 4 3 2
♣ Q 6 5

West	North	East	South
1 ♡	Pass	Pass	1 ♠
2 ♣	2 ♠	3 ♡	3 ♣
All Pass			

Opening Lead: ♡ 6

1. Dummy plays low at trick one. Which heart do you play?
2. What do you make of the distribution around the table judging from the bidding and the opening lead?

NO PROBLEM (SOLUTION)

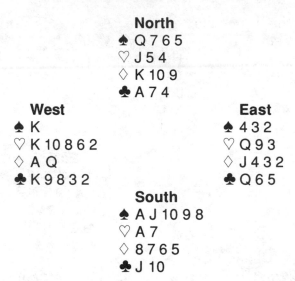

North
♠ Q 7 6 5
♡ J 5 4
◇ K 10 9
♣ A 7 4

West
♠ K
♡ K 10 8 6 2
◇ A Q
♣ K 9 8 3 2

East
♠ 4 3 2
♡ Q 9 3
◇ J 4 3 2
♣ Q 6 5

South
♠ A J 10 9 8
♡ A 7
◇ 8 7 6 5
♣ J 10

1.   The ♡ 9. Declarer must have the ♡ A and partner the ♡ K. Partner has shown no more than five hearts from the lead and you must hope partner has the ♡ 10 as well. If you play the ♡ Q, declarer can lead back the ♡ J and eventually get a discard.

Playing the ♡ Q only works when declarer has specifically ♡ A 10 and cannot use a discard on the ♡ J. A long shot.

2.   Partner is known to have five hearts and at least four clubs. South must have at least five spades. Therefore, partner's distribution could be either 1-5-3-4 or 1-5-2-5. With the first distribution he would have doubled 1 ♠ for takeout, so assume the second. If declarer does not work out the trump position, down he goes.

KEY LESSON POINTERS

1.   HOLDING Q9x, K9x, Q9xx OR K9xx OVER Jxx IN THE DUMMY, IT IS ALMOST AL-WAYS RIGHT TO INSERT THE NINE WHEN PARTNER LEADS LOW VS. A SUIT CONTRACT. DECLARER WILL HAVE THE ACE, AND PARTNER WILL USUALLY HAVE THE OTHER MISSING HONOR. THE ONLY TIME TO VIOLATE THIS RULE IS WHEN ONE NEEDS A QUICK TRICK IN THE SUIT.

2.   WHEN PARTNER CAN HAVE ONE OF TWO POSSIBLE DISTRIBUTIONS, ASSIGN HIM THE ONE THAT HE IS MORE APT TO HAVE ON THE BIDDING. HERE, FOR EXAMPLE, WEST IS MORE APT TO BE 5-5 IN HEARTS AND CLUBS THAN 1-5-3-4. WITH THAT DISTRIBUTION HE WOULD HAVE BEEN MORE LIKELY TO MAKE A TAKEOUT DOUBLE.

(27) BACK AND FORTH

North-South vulnerable
Dealer East

North
♠ A 9 6 4
♡ –
◇ K J 9 8
♣ K J 4 3 2

East (you)
♠ K Q J 10 8 3
♡ 9 6
◇ 5 3 2
♣ Q 8

East	South	West	North
2 ♠	3 ♡	Pass	3 ♠
Pass	4 ◇	Pass	6 ◇
All Pass			

Opening Lead: ♠ 5

Declarer wins the ♠ A and immediately ruffs a spade with the ◇ 6. Declarer continues with the ♡ A and a low heart, ruffing with the ◇ 8. Partner follows suit up the line.

Next, declarer crosses to the ♣ A, partner playing the ♣ 7, and ruffs another heart with the ◇ 9. What do you do?

BACK AND FORTH (SOLUTION)

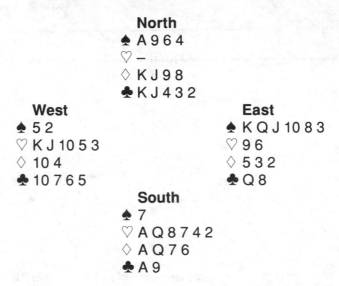

North
♠ A 9 6 4
♡ —
♢ K J 9 8
♣ K J 4 3 2

West
♠ 5 2
♡ K J 10 5 3
♢ 10 4
♣ 10 7 6 5

East
♠ K Q J 10 8 3
♡ 9 6
♢ 5 3 2
♣ Q 8

South
♠ 7
♡ A Q 8 7 4 2
♢ A Q 7 6
♣ A 9

Discard the ♣ Q to stop the crossruff. Partner has given you a count in every suit so you know that declarer has only two clubs.

If you do not discard the ♣ Q, declarer will have no trouble crossruffing for twelve tricks — and you can see it coming: two clubs, two major aces, and eight trump tricks.

In other circumstances your play might be dangerous if it establishes the entire club suit, but here, with partner marked with four clubs, it is mandatory.

KEY LESSON POINTERS

1. WHEN DECLARER EMBARKS ON A CROSSRUFF AND NEGLECTS TO CASH HIS TOP CARDS IN THE OFF SUITS, A DEFENDER SHOULD BE ON THE LOOKOUT TO SHORTEN HIMSELF IN ONE OF THESE SUITS SO THAT DECLARER CANNOT CASH HIS WINNER(S) LATER.

2. THE DISCARD OF AN IMPORTANT HONOR THAT ESTABLISHES AN ENTIRE SUIT FOR DECLARER WHILE HE CAN STILL DRAW TRUMPS AND USE THE SUIT IS OUT OF THE QUESTION. THAT IS NOT THE CASE HERE. THE CLUBS WILL NOT BE GOOD AFTER THE DISCARD OF THE ♣ Q.

3. INCIDENTALLY, DO YOU SEE HOW DECLARER COULD STILL MAKE THE HAND IF HIS REMAINING CLUB WAS THE TEN INSTEAD OF THE NINE AFTER THE DISCARD OF THE ♣ Q? ANSWER BELOW.
   ALL DECLARER HAS TO DO IS DRAW THREE ROUNDS OF TRUMP. WEST MUST DISCARD A HEART AND SOUTH CAN EITHER GIVE UP A HEART, USING THE ♣ 10 AS A REENTRY, OR CASH THE ♣ 10 AND CONCEDE A HEART FORCING WEST TO GIVE DUMMY THE LEAD WHERE ALL THE GOOD CLUBS RESIDE.

(28) FANCY BIDDING

Both sides vulnerable
Dealer South

North
♠ A 4
♡ A Q 2
♢ Q 10 6 5
♣ K 10 9 8

East (you)
♠ K 9 8 3
♡ J 4
♢ J 9 7 2
♣ 7 6 5

South	West	North	East
1 NT	Pass	4 NT	Pass
6 ♡*	All Pass		

*Five card suit plus maximum

Opening Lead: ♠ 2 (Third or fifth best)

Declarer plays the ♠ A and you signal with the ♠ 9. Declarer plays the ♡ A Q and exits with dummy's ♠ 4.
1.   Which spade do you play? If you play the ♠ K, what do you return?

FANCY BIDDING (SOLUTION)

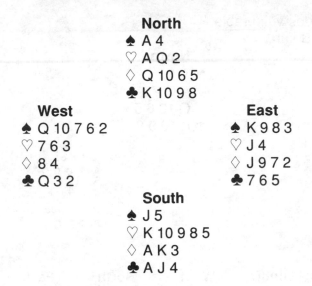

North
♠ A 4
♡ A Q 2
◇ Q 10 6 5
♣ K 10 9 8

West
♠ Q 10 7 6 2
♡ 7 6 3
◇ 8 4
♣ Q 3 2

East
♠ K 9 8 3
♡ J 4
◇ J 9 7 2
♣ 7 6 5

South
♠ J 5
♡ K 10 9 8 5
◇ A K 3
♣ A J 4

1.   You should duck the trick. You assume your partner has led from a five card spade suit. (If declarer had four spades he wouldn't be playing the hand this way.)

If you don't duck, what are you going to return upon winning the ♠ K? Chances are either minor suit lead will cost a trick, and a spade will be a ruff and a sluff.   The better chance is to play low and hope your partner has the ♠ Q. If so, your partner will have the last trump with which to exit safely.

If you defend passively and avoid leading either minor suit, declarer will have to locate the ♣ Q by his lonesome.

KEY LESSON POINTERS

1. EVEN IF YOU DON'T LEAD LOW FROM ODD AND THIRD BEST FROM EVEN, FAMILIAR-IZE YOURSELF WITH THE CONVENTION. MANY OF YOUR OPPONENTS WILL BE US-ING IT.
2. ALTHOUGH IT ISN'T WRITTEN IN STONE, WHEN DECLARER WINS THE OPENING LEAD IN DUMMY WITH THE ACE AND YOU, THIRD HAND, HAVE THE KING, PARTNER, NOT DECLARER USUALLY HAS THE QUEEN.
3. A PASSIVE DEFENSE AGAINST TWO BALANCED HANDS IS USUALLY BEST. TRY TO AVOID BREAKING NEW SUITS. LET DECLARER HAVE THAT HONOR. IT IS ONE HE IS NOT LOOKING FOR.

(29) MORE INSULTS

Neither side vulnerable
Dealer South

> **North**
> ♠ K 9 5
> ♡ K 9
> ◇ A Q J 5
> ♣ 10 9 3 2

>> **East (you)**
>> ♠ Q 8 7 6
>> ♡ J 10 4 3
>> ◇ 4
>> ♣ K Q 7 6

South	West	North	East
1 ◇	Pass	2 NT	Pass
4 NT	Pass	6 ◇	All Pass

Opening Lead: ◇ 2

Declarer wins the first two tricks with the jack and ace of diamonds. You discard a spade on the second diamond.

Declarer continues with the ♠ A, a spade to the king, and a spade ruff. Next comes the ♡ A and the ♡ Q to dummy.

At this point the ♣ 10 is led from dummy. What is declarer's distribution, and which club do you play?

MORE INSULTS (SOLUTION)

North
♠ K 9 5
♡ K 9
◇ A Q J 5
♣ 10 9 3 2

West
♠ J 4 3 2
♡ 8 7 6 5 2
◇ 9 2
♣ J 4

East
♠ Q 8 7 6
♡ J 10 4 3
◇ 4
♣ K Q 7 6

South
♠ A 10
♡ A Q
◇ K 10 8 7 6 3
♣ A 8 5

Declarer is almost certain to be 2-2-6-3 and you must play low hoping partner has the ♣ J.

If you cover, declarer wins and plays a second club to partner's jack. Partner now has to concede a ruff and a sluff and declarer makes the unmakeable slam.

KEY LESSON POINTERS

1. IF YOU DO NOT COUNT DECLARER'S HAND ON DEFENSE, YOU CAN FOLD UP YOUR TENT AND GO HOME. YOU ARE SIMPLY NOT GOING TO KNOW WHAT TO DO AT THE END OF THE HAND — NOT TO MENTION THE BEGINNING OR THE MIDDLE.

2. ONCE YOU HAVE COUNTED DECLARER'S HAND, YOUR TASK IS NOT OVER. IF IT BOILS DOWN TO A ONE SUIT PROBLEM, AS IT DOES HERE, YOU MUST ASK YOUR-SELF HOW MANY TRICKS YOU NEED FROM THIS SUIT, AND THE MINIMUM PARTNER MUST HAVE FOR YOU TO REALIZE THESE TRICKS. THEN PLAY ACCORDINGLY.

3. ON MOST OF THE HANDS THAT DECLARER STRIPS BEFORE ATTACKING THE CRITI-CAL SUIT, YOU SHOULD BE ABLE TO GET A COUNT ON THE OFF SUITS WHETHER OR NOT PARTNER GIVES YOU COUNT SIGNALS.

4. MOST EXPERTS DO NOT GIVE MANY COUNT SIGNALS IN SLAM CONTRACTS. THE FEELING IS THAT DECLARER BENEFITS MORE THAN PARTNER. PARTNER IS SUP-POSED TO BE ABLE TO WORK OUT THE DISTRIBUTION FROM THE BIDDING AND THE WAY DECLARER ATTACKS THE HAND. SURELY YOU PLAY WITH PARTNERS WHO HAVE NO TROUBLE DOING THAT.

(30) PLAYING COY (2)

East-West vulnerable
Dealer South

North
♠ A 6 4
♡ A Q 8 7 6
◊ K 5
♣ 10 4 3

West (you)
♠ Q 10 5 2
♡ K 3
◊ 8 7 6
♣ A J 5 2

South	West	North	East
1 ◊	Pass	1 ♡	Pass
2 ♣	Pass	2 ♣	Pass
3 ♣	Pass	3 ◊	Pass
3 ♡	Pass	4 ♣	Pass
5 ♣	All Pass		

Opening Lead: ♠ 2

1.   Declarer wins the ♠ A in dummy, partner encourages with the ♠ 9. From the bidding and the play to the first trick, what do you make of declarer's distribution?
2.   Declarer continues with a low club to the king.
      What do you do?
      Play low. It is almost always right to duck with AJxx in back of the KQ the first time the suit is led. It usually forces declarer to waste an entry to lead up to the queen; and it also gives him a false sense of security.
3.   Declarer continues with a low diamond to the king and then plays a low club from dummy, partner discarding a spade. When declarer inserts the ♣ 9 you win the ♣ J and play a second spade which declarer ruffs.
      Declarer continues with the ace and queen of diamonds, all following, and then produces the ◊ J. What is your plan? (At this point you remain with two spades, two hearts and two trumps. Dummy has a spade, four hearts to the AQ, and the ♣ 10.)

PLAYING COY (SOLUTION)

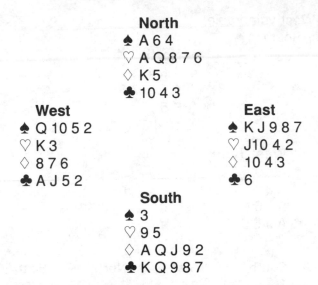

North
♠ A 6 4
♡ A Q 8 7 6
◇ K 5
♣ 10 4 3

West
♠ Q 10 5 2
♡ K 3
◇ 8 7 6
♣ A J 5 2

East
♠ K J 9 8 7
♡ J10 4 2
◇ 10 4 3
♣ 6

South
♠ 3
♡ 9 5
◇ A Q J 9 2
♣ K Q 9 8 7

1.   Declarer is bidding and playing like someone with 1-2-5-5 distribution.

3.   Declarer has erred and you should take advantage. Discard a heart on the fourth diamond and your last heart on the fifth diamond.

Once you have unloaded <u>one</u> heart, declarer has lost control of the hand. If he plays hearts after running the diamonds you will ruff. If he plays a trump, you will win, and play a spade forcing out his last trump. Either way he is a cooked goose.

KEY LESSON POINTERS

1.   SOMETIMES THE BIDDING IS SO REVEALING YOU WILL KNOW DECLARER'S DISTRI- BUTION BEFORE A SINGLE CARD HAS BEEN PLAYED.

2.   WHEN FACED WITH THE DILEMMA OF DECLARER PLAYING A LONG SUIT THROUGH YOU, CONSIDER HOW THE PLAY WILL DEVELOP IF YOU (a) RUFF HIGH; (b) RUFF LOW; (c) DISCARD. ONCE YOU HAVE GONE THROUGH ALL THE POSSIBILITIES, WAKE EVERYBODY UP WHEN YOU ARE FINALLY READY TO PLAY.

(31) FAN.... TASTIC

North-South vulnerable
Dealer South

North
♠ K Q
♡ 4
◇ 8 7 6 3 2
♣ J 8 5 3 2

West (you)
♠ A 8 2
♡ K 10 2
◇ K 9 5 4
♣ 10 6 4

South	West	North	East
1 ♡	Pass	1 NT	Pass
3 ♡	All Pass		

Opening Lead: ◇ 4

Partner's ◇ J drives out declarer's ◇ A. At trick two declarer leads the ♠ 9 to the queen, which you duck, partner playing the ♠ 3.

A trump is led from dummy to declarer's queen and your king. Now what?

FAN.... TASTIC (SOLUTION)

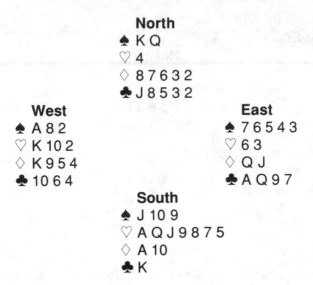

North
♠ K Q
♡ 4
♢ 8 7 6 3 2
♣ J 8 5 3 2

West
♠ A 8 2
♡ K 10 2
♢ K 9 5 4
♣ 10 6 4

East
♠ 7 6 5 4 3
♡ 6 3
♢ Q J
♣ A Q 9 7

South
♠ J 10 9
♡ A Q J 9 8 7 5
♢ A 10
♣ K

Declarer is known to have three spades (probably headed by the jack because he failed to try for a spade ruff), the ace-ten of diamonds doubleton, six or seven hearts, and a club holding that he does not have to lead up to. (With one dummy entry, declarer would have opted to take a 50-50 proposition in clubs rather than an inferior percentage play in hearts.)

After all is said and done, there are at least two possible defenses that will set the contract. Defense I: Lead a club to partner's presumed ace. If partner returns a diamond, you can either overtake, cash the ♠ A, and lead a low diamond hoping partner can uppercut with the ♡ 9, or duck the ♢ Q, win the spade return and lead the ♢ 9. Partner should ruff this trick. If it happens to be with the ♡ 9, you have promoted your ♡ 10 to the setting trick. This defense requires partner to have the ♣ A and the ♡ 9.

Defense II: Lead a low spade after winning the ♡ K! This is not a misprint. Locked in dummy, what can declarer do? If he leads a club, partner wins the ace and leads a spade to your ace; you underlead your ♢ K to his ♢ Q, and when partner returns a fourth round of spades you make your ♡ 10. This line of defense requires only that partner have the ♣ A. Fan... tastic.

KEY LESSON POINTERS

1. SOMETIMES ONE HAS TO USE THE BIDDING, THE PLAY TO THE FIRST TRICK, THE CHOICE OF SPOTS CARDS THAT DECLARER OPTS TO USE, PARTNER'S COUNT SIGNAL, AND A LITTLE IMAGINATION TO DEFEAT THE CONTRACT.
2. IF YOU DID NOT FIND THE RIGHT DEFENSE TO DEFEAT THIS CONTRACT, DON'T FEEL BAD. ANYONE WHO DID SHOULD NOT BE READING THIS BOOK. HE SHOULD BE WRITING ONE OF HIS OWN.

(32) READING THE POSITION

East-West vulnerable
Dealer South

North
♠ 10 6
♡ 10 4 3
◇ K 10
♣ A J 10 5 4 3

East (you)
♠ Q 9 8 5
♡ 7 5
◇ 9 7 6 5 2
♣ K Q

South	West	North	East
1 NT	Pass	3 NT	All Pass

Opening Lead: ♡ Q

1.   Which heart do you play at trick one?
2.   Declarer wins the ♡ K. Who has the ♡ A?
3.   At trick two declarer leads a club to the A and a club back, as partner discards the ♡ 9. On lead in clubs, what do you return at trick four?

READING THE POSITION (SOLUTION)

North
♠ 10 6
♡ 10 4 3
♢ K 10
♣ A J 10 5 4 3

West
♠ A J 4 2
♡ Q J 9 8 2
♢ Q 4 3
♣ 7

East
♠ Q 9 8 5
♡ 7 5
♢ 9 7 6 5 2
♣ K Q

South
♠ K 7 3
♡ A K 6
♢ A J 8
♣ 9 8 6 2

1.   The ♡ 5, attitude.
2.   You can't be 100% sure. Partner could be leading from a combination headed by either the QJ9 or the AQJ.
3.   The ♠ Q. Partner has told you not to return a heart. If he wanted a heart return, he wouldn't have discarded one. As he had a choice of hearts to discard, and he selected a rather high one, you should assume that it is a suit preference discard and shift to a spade. You shift to the ♠ Q because you are playing for four spade tricks and you have to find partner with ♠ AJxx. If he has those cards, you cannot afford shift to a low spade lest declarer duck the trick around to the ten.

KEY LESSON POINTERS

1.   GIVE ATTITUDE, NOT COUNT, WHEN PARTNER LEADS AN HONOR VS. NOTRUMP.
2.   WHEN PARTNER DISCARDS FROM THE SAME SUIT THAT HE HAS LED VS. NO TRUMP, THE INFERENCE IS THAT HE DOES NOT WANT THAT SUIT RETURNED. OFTEN HE CAN TELL YOU BY THE SIZE OF THE CARD HE HAS DISCARDED WHICH SUIT HE DOES WANT.
3.   WHEN THE DUMMY TO YOUR RIGHT HAS 10x AND YOU HAVE Qxxx OR Jxxx, AND YOU NEED FOUR FAST TRICKS IN THE SUIT, SHIFT TO YOUR HONOR, PLAYING PARTNER FOR FOUR CARDS TO TWO HIGH HONORS INCLUDING THE ACE AND THE NINE. OF COURSE, IF YOU HAVE THE NINE PARTNER ONLY NEEDS TWO HONORS INCLUDING THE ACE.

(33) HIDDEN FIT

East-West vulnerable
Dealer North

> **North**
> ♠ 9 7 4 2
> ♡ A K Q J 5
> ◇ K 7 2
> ♣ K

West (you)
♠ K
♡ 9 4
◇ A J 8
♣ Q J 9 7 6 3 2

North	East	South	West
2 ◇*	Pass	4 ♠	All Pass

*Five hearts and four spades, 11-15 H.C.P.

Opening Lead: ♣ Q

Declarer ruffs the opening lead and plays the ♠ Q to your king. What do you return at trick three?

HIDDEN FIT (SOLUTION)

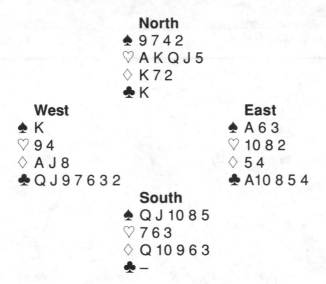

North
♠ 9 7 4 2
♡ A K Q J 5
♢ K 7 2
♣ K

West
♠ K
♡ 9 4
♢ A J 8
♣ Q J 9 7 6 3 2

East
♠ A 6 3
♡ 10 8 2
♢ 5 4
♣ A10 8 5 4

South
♠ Q J 10 8 5
♡ 7 6 3
♢ Q 10 9 6 3
♣ —

A low diamond. Partner is marked with the trump ace and declarer's distribution must be either 5-4-4-0, 5-3-5-0, 6-4-3-0, or 6-3-4-0, or 6-2-5-0.

Anytime declarer has six spades you must shift to a diamond hoping partner has the queen. If you don't, declarer will discard diamonds on hearts and eventually lead up to the ♢ K. If declarer has six spades and the ♢ Q, there is no defense.

If declarer has five spades and four hearts, it is right to shift to a heart as partner has a singleton and can easily get a ruff upon gaining the lead with the ♠ A and shifting to a diamond.

Finally, if declarer has the distribution you see, you can defeat the contract by shifting to a low diamond, and later giving your partner a diamond ruff when he gains the lead with the ♠ A.

As the low diamond shift works out much more often than the heart shift, it is clearly indicated.

KEY LESSON POINTERS

1. TRY TO WORK OUT DECLARER'S DISTRIBUTION BEFORE YOU MAKE ANY RASH PLAYS.
2. WHEN DECLARER CAN HAVE A NUMBER OF DISTRIBUTIONS, CATER TO THE MOST LIKELY ONES. HERE, A HEART SHIFT IS ONLY RIGHT IF DECLARER STARTED WITH FOUR HEARTS AND FIVE SPADES. WITH THAT DISTRIBUTION HE MIGHT HAVE LEAPED TO 4 ♡ RATHER THAN 4 ♠.
3. ALTHOUGH YOU MAY STILL DEFEAT THE CONTRACT IF YOU SHIFT TO A HEART, (DECLARER MAY MISGUESS THE DIAMOND POSITION) WHY PUT YOURSELF IN THAT POSITION WHEN YOU HAVE AN EASY BEAT?

(34) AM I ENDPLAYED, OR WHAT?

North-South vulnerable
Dealer South

North
♠ K J 10 7 6
♡ J 10 3 2
◇ 7 4
♣ K 4

West (you)
♠ 9 8
♡ Q 9 7
◇ Q 10 9 3
♣ 10 9 8 7

South	West	North	East
1 NT	Pass	2 ♣	Pass
2 ♠	Pass	3 ♠	Pass
4 ♠	All Pass		

Opening Lead: ♣ 10

Partner wins the first two tricks with the ♣ J and ♣ A and shifts to the ◇ 8. Declarer wins the ◇ A, cashes the ♠ A and leads a spade to the king felling partner's doubleton queen.

At trick six, declarer runs the ♡ J to your queen, partner playing the ♡ 4 and declarer the ♡ 5.
What do you play to trick seven?

AM I ENDPLAYED, OR WHAT? (SOLUTION)

North
♠ K J 10 7 6
♡ J 10 3 2
♢ 7 4
♣ K 4

West
♠ 9 8
♡ Q 9 7
♢ Q 10 9 3
♣ 10 9 8 7

East
♠ Q 5
♡ K 6 4
♢ 8 6 5
♣ A Q J 5 2

South
♠ A 4 3 2
♡ A 8 5
♢ A K J 2
♣ 6 3

Your only truly safe return is a diamond — even though you know that declarer has the KJ. After all, what good is one discard going to do for him?

Both a club and a heart lead are fraught with danger. A club may well be a ruff and a sluff, and a heart may cost you the setting trick if declarer has the ♡ A 8.

As your only possible remaining defensive trick must come from the heart suit, and as a diamond return is completely safe, lead one!

KEY LESSON POINTERS

1. WHEN FACED WITH A CHOICE OF APPARENTLY LOSING OPTIONS, LEAD THE SUIT THAT IS LEAST LIKELY TO BE HARMFUL TO YOUR SIDE.
2. LEADING INTO A TENACE POSITION IS NOT FATAL IF DECLARER HAS NO USEFUL DISCARD TO TAKE ON AN ESTABLISHED WINNER.
3. THE HEART SUIT IS WORTHY OF STUDY. AFTER THE JACK OF HEARTS LOSES TO WEST, NO ONE CAN PLAY HEARTS SAFELY. IT IS A SUIT THAT YOU WANT YOUR OPPONENTS TO PLAY, NOT YOU.
4. YES, DECLARER CAN ALWAYS MAKE THE HAND IF HE RUFFS A DIAMOND BEFORE PLAYING TRUMPS, THEN PLAYS THE KING AND ACE OF SPADES ENDING IN HIS HAND, RUFFS HIS LAST DIAMOND AND RUNS THE ♡ J. NOW YOU ARE TRULY ENDPLAYED; YOU MUST EXIT WITH THE ♡ 7, AND IF DECLARER GUESSES TO PLAY LOW FROM DUMMY HE WILL MAKE 4 ♠.

(35) MY TRICK?

North-South vulnerable
Dealer West

             North
             ♠ J 6 3
             ♡ A K Q J
             ◇ A K 8 7 6
             ♣ A

   West (you)
   ♠ K Q 10 9 8 7
   ♡ 4 3
   ◇ Q J
   ♣ 7 6 5

West	North	East	South
2 ♠*	Dbl.	Pass	3 NT
Pass	6 NT	All Pass	
* Weak			

   Opening Lead: ♠ K

Your King holds the trick, partner playing the ♠ 4, declarer the ♠ 5. Now what?

MY TRICK? (SOLUTION)

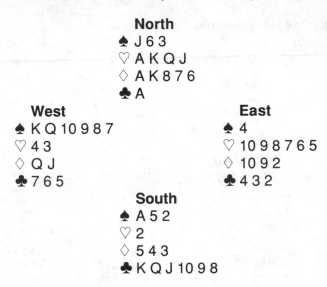

North
♠ J 6 3
♡ A K Q J
◇ A K 8 7 6
♣ A

West
♠ K Q 10 9 8 7
♡ 4 3
◇ Q J
♣ 7 6 5

East
♠ 4
♡ 10 9 8 7 6 5
◇ 10 9 2
♣ 4 3 2

South
♠ A 5 2
♡ 2
◇ 5 4 3
♣ K Q J 10 9 8

Did you return the queen. . . of spades? You should have. What can declarer possibly have for his leap to 3 NT other than the ♠ A and great clubs?
How is he going to use those clubs? Right, by cashing the ♣ A and coming to his hand with the ♠ A. But not if you knock out the ♠ A at trick two. Then, all you need is for your partner to have the ◇ 10 so that declarer cannot enter his hand with a diamond after cashing the ◇ A K. Did you diagnose the position? What an analyst you are!

KEY LESSON POINTERS

1. MANY PLAYERS LEAD THE Q FROM KQ10 COMBINATIONS VS. NOTRUMP. PARTNER IS SUPPOSED TO UNLOAD THE JACK IF HE HAS IT, AND SIGNAL ENCOURAGEMENT WITH THE ACE. WITH SMALL CARDS, THIRD HAND PLAYS LOW. WHEN THIRD HAND CANNOT POSSIBLY HAVE THE ACE ON THE BIDDING, HE GIVES COUNT WITH HIS SMALL CARDS.
2. WHEN IT IS OBVIOUS FROM THE SIGHT OF THE DUMMY THAT DECLARER HAS A LONG CONCEALED SUIT THAT IS BLOCKED, THE DEFENSE MUST TRY TO REMOVE THE ENTRY TO THE BLOCKED SUIT AS SOON AS POSSIBLE.
3. NINETY-NINE TIMES OUT OF 100 WHEN YOU LEAD THE KING FROM A KING-QUEEN COMBINATION AND THE GUARDED JACK IS IN THE DUMMY, DECLARER WILL WIN THE ACE, IF HE HAS IT, TO INSURE A SECOND TRICK IN THE SUIT. NOT THIS TIME.

(36) BLACKWOOD SIGNOFF

Neither side vulnerable
Dealer East

North
♠ A K Q 6 4
♡ K 9 8 4
◇ J
♣ K J 5

West (you)
♠ 10 3
♡ –
◇ 9 7 4 2
♣ A Q 9 8 7 6 2

East	South	West	North
Pass	1 ♡	3 ♣*	4 NT
Pass	5 ◇	Pass	5 ♡
All Pass			
*Weak			

Opening Lead: ♣ A

Partner plays the ♣ 4 and declarer the ♣ 10. What do you play at trick two?

BLACKWOOD SIGNOFF (SOLUTION)

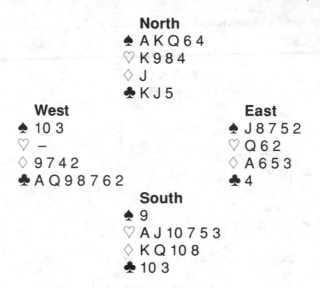

North
♠ A K Q 6 4
♡ K 9 8 4
◇ J
♣ K J 5

West
♠ 10 3
♡ −
◇ 9 7 4 2
♣ A Q 9 8 7 6 2

East
♠ J 8 7 5 2
♡ Q 6 2
◇ A 6 5 3
♣ 4

South
♠ 9
♡ A J 10 7 5 3
◇ K Q 10 8
♣ 10 3

Your best chance is to hope that declarer is falsecarding in clubs and that partner has a singleton. If he does, he will ruff your club return and score whichever red ace he happens to hold.

Can a club return ever lose? Yes, but it would take a remote possibility. If declarer has specifically: Jx   A10xxxx   KQxx x he can insert the ♣ J, play two rounds of trumps, discard two more diamonds on the third and fourth winning spades, and finally play either the ♣ K or the fifth spade to discard his last diamond. Partner goes to bed with the ◇ A and scores only one trump trick. Clearly, the best chance is to try to give partner a club ruff.

KEY LESSON POINTERS

1. WHEN TWO LINES OF DEFENSE PRESENT THEMSELVES, AND ONE REQUIRES A SIMPLE POSSIBILITY, THE OTHER A REMOTE POSSIBILITY, GO FOR THE SIMPLE LINE. YOUR PARTNERS WILL LOVE YOU FOR IT.

2. WHENEVER THE OPPONENTS LAUNCH INTO BLACKWOOD AND SUBSIDE AT THE FIVE LEVEL, ASSUME YOUR SIDE HAS TWO ACES. HOWEVER, IF THE OPPONENTS ARE PLAYING KEY CARD BLACKWOOD YOUR SIDE MIGHT HAVE ONE ACE AND THE KING OF TRUMPS, OR EVEN ONE ACE AND THE QUEEN OF TRUMPS.

3. WHEN PARTNER LEADS THE ACE OF A SUIT IN WHICH HE HAS SHOWN GREAT LENGTH AND THE DUMMY COMES DOWN WITH STRENGTH IN THAT SUIT, THIRD HAND SHOULD GIVE COUNT. IF THIRD HAND HAS SUPPORTED THE SUIT, THIRD HAND SHOULD MAKE A SUIT PREFERENCE SIGNAL AS IT IS OBVIOUS TO BOTH SIDES THAT THE SUIT SHOULD NOT BE CONTINUED.

(37) STUCK! (1)   (2)

East-West vulnerable
Dealer South

North
♠ J 2
♡ A K 10 6 4
◇ Q 4
♣ A Q J 4

West (you)
♠ K 10 8
♡ Q J 2
◇ K 9 7 6
♣ K 6 3

South	West	North	East
2 ♠	Pass	4 ♠	All Pass

Opening Lead: ◇ 6

Partner wins the ◇ A and returns the ◇ 3 to your king, declarer playing the ten and jack.
1.   What do you lead to trick three?
   The ♡ 2.
2.   Declarer wins the ♡ A, partner plays the ♡ 9, dummy runs the ♠ J, partner playing the ♠ 5. Now what?
   You duck the trick — casually.
3.   Declarer continues with a spade to his queen, partner playing the ♠ 6. Now what?

STUCK!   (SOLUTION)

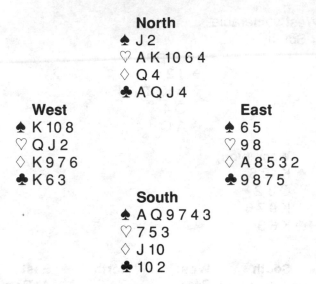

North
♠ J 2
♡ A K 10 6 4
◊ Q 4
♣ A Q J 4

West
♠ K 10 8
♡ Q J 2
◊ K 9 7 6
♣ K 6 3

East
♠ 6 5
♡ 9 8
◊ A 8 5 3 2
♣ 9 8 7 5

South
♠ A Q 9 7 4 3
♡ 7 5 3
◊ J 10
♣ 10 2

3.   Now you have declarer where you want him. You win the ♠ K and stick him in dummy with the ♡ Q. Unable to get to his hand to take the winning club finesse, declarer must go down one.

KEY LESSON POINTERS

1. WHEN LOOKING AT AK10 IN THE DUMMY TO YOUR LEFT, LEAD LOW FROM ANY QUEEN-JACK COMBINATION MOST OF THE TIME. DECLARER WILL SELDOM, IF EVER, PLAY THE TEN AND NEXT TIME YOU WILL BE ABLE TO LEAD AN HONOR SAFELY.

2. WHEN DUMMY HAS TWO TRUMPS AND DECLARER IS SHORT OF HAND ENTRIES TO TAKE WINNING FINESSES, IT IS A GOOD PLAY TO WIN THE SECOND ROUND OF TRUMPS RATHER THAN THE FIRST. DECLARER MAY THEN HAVE AN H... OF A TIME GETTING BACK TO HIS HAND TO: (a) DRAW TRUMPS; (b) TAKE THOSE WINNING FINESSES.

3. IF YOU SUSPECT YOUR PARTNER HAS LED FROM SHORTNESS, YOUR RETURN SHOULD BE SUIT PREFERENCE NOT COUNT. IN CASE PARTNER RUFFS, HE WANTS TO KNOW WHICH SUIT TO RETURN, NOT HOW MANY CARDS YOU HAVE IN THE SUIT.

(38) CHEESY OPENING

North-South vulnerable
Dealer West

North
♠ 9 8 2
♡ 10 4 3
◇ A K 6 5
♣ 7 4 3

West (you)
♠ Q 6 4 3
♡ Q J 7
◇ 9 4 3
♣ A K 10

West	North	East	South
1 ♣	Pass	2 ♣	Dbl.
Pass	2 ◇	Pass	2 ♠
Pass	3 ♠	Pass	4 ♠
All Pass			

Opening Lead:　♣ K

Partner plays the ♣ Q and you continue with the ace and a club, declarer ruffing with the ♠ 10. At trick four declarer exits with the ♠ J.

What do you make of this strange play, and what do you do?

CHEESY OPENING   (SOLUTION)

North
♠ 9 8 2
♡ 10 4 3
◇ A K 6 5
♣ 7 4 3

West
♠ Q 6 4 3
♡ Q J 7
◇ 9 4 3
♣ A K 10

East
♠ 5
♡ 9 8 2
◇ 10 8 7 2
♣ Q J 9 8 6

South
♠ A K J 10 7
♡ A K 6 5
◇ Q J
♣ 5 2

For openers, South has bid the hand very strongly and should have all of the missing high cards, save, perhaps, the ◇ J.

So what kind of a play is this? There are two possibilities:

(1) South is guarding against a 4-1 spade division holding:

AKJ107   AKx   QJx   xx

If South bangs down the ♠ A K and finds four spades in one hand he could lose control. If the player with four spades has four clubs, he can force South to ruff with his last trump upon winning the ♠ Q. The defender's last trump now becomes the setting trick.

If South has the pictured hand, you cannot set the contract, so think of something else.

(2) An even more likely possiblity is that South is trying to create a trump entry to dummy because the diamonds are blocked. This play would succeed if trumps were 3-2, but you know they are not.

You can afford to give South the dummy entry because you hold four spades and three diamonds. He will not be able to discard <u>two</u> hearts on the diamonds before you ruff in. Your play is to win the ♠ Q and exit with any card in your hand other than a low heart. You will always come to a heart trick. If you duck this trick, South can make the hand.

He will cash a high spade, see the division, and shift gears. He will cash three diamonds and then ace-king and a heart giving you the lead. You will: (1) have to lead away from your guarded ♠ Q; (2) have plenty of explaining to do.

KEY LESSON POINTERS

1. WHEN DECLARER MAKES AN UNUSUAL PLAY, ASK YOURSELF WHAT HE HAS IN MIND.

2. IF SEVERAL POSSIBILITIES PRESENT THEMSELVES, PICK THE ONE THAT ALLOWS YOU TO DEFEAT THE CONTRACT AND ELIMINATE THE OTHERS.

3 WHEN AN OPPONENT DOUBLES AND THEN BIDS A SUIT, ASSUME HE HAS A MINIMUM OF 17 HIGH CARD POINTS — A LITTLE LESS IF HE DOESN'T READ BRIDGE BOOKS.

(39) LOCK IT UP

East-West vulnerable
Dealer South

North
♠ Q 10 9 8 7
♡ Q 9 8 7
◇ 2
♣ A J 10

East (you)
♠ 4
♡ A K J 10 6 5
◇ A 10
♣ K 7 4 3

South	West	North	East
1 NT	Pass	2 ♣	2 ♡
2 ♠	Pass	4 ♠	All Pass

Opening Lead: ♡ 4

Dummy plays low, and you win the first trick with the ♡ 10. Now what?

LOCK IT UP (SOLUTION)

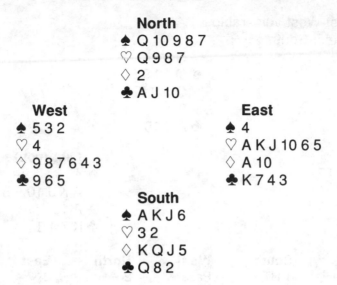

North
♠ Q 10 9 8 7
♡ Q 9 8 7
♢ 2
♣ A J 10

West
♠ 5 3 2
♡ 4
♢ 9 8 7 6 4 3
♣ 9 6 5

East
♠ 4
♡ A K J 10 6 5
♢ A 10
♣ K 7 4 3

South
♠ A K J 6
♡ 3 2
♢ K Q J 5
♣ Q 8 2

Lead your lowest heart for partner to ruff. His club return will give declarer no chance to avoid four losers. You will lose your club trick on declarer's diamonds if you don't defend this way.

KEY LESSON POINTERS

1. WHEN THERE IS A DEFENSE THAT WILL CLEARLY DEFEAT THE CONTRACT, YOU HAD BETTER BE PRETTY SURE OF YOURSELF IF YOU DON'T OPT TO TAKE IT.
2. WHENEVER YOU GIVE YOUR PARTNER A RUFF IN A SUIT IN WHICH YOU ARE KNOWN TO HAVE LENGTH, YOUR CARD IS A SUIT PREFERENCE SIGNAL. HAD YOU WANTED YOUR PARTNER TO RETURN A DIAMOND AFTER RUFFING THE HEART, YOU WOULD HAVE RETURNED A HIGH HEART.
3. YOU HAVE 15 HIGH CARD POINTS AND DUMMY HAS 9 FOR A TOTAL OF 24. DECLAR-ER IS KNOWN TO HAVE 15-17, SO THE VERY MOST YOUR PARTNER CAN HOLD IS A JACK. YOU SHOULD GET IN THE HABIT OF ASSESSING YOUR PARTNER'S STRENGTH BY USING THIS TECHNIQUE EVERY TIME THE DUMMY COMES DOWN.

(40) YOU'RE JOKING, OF COURSE

Both sides vulnerable
Dealer South

North
♠ Q J 6 4
♡ A 9 3
◇ 10 9 2
♣ A 7 4

East (you)
♠ A 10 9 8
♡ 7
◇ 8 7 6 3
♣ K 10 6 2

South	West	North	East
1 ♡	Pass	1 ♠	Pass
3 ♡	Pass	4 ♡	All Pass

Opening Lead: ♣ Q

Dummy plays low.
1. Who has the ♣ J?
2. Which club do you play at trick one?
3. What is your plan?

YOU'RE JOKING, OF COURSE (SOLUTION)

North
♠ Q J 6 4
♡ A 9 3
◇ 10 9 2
♣ A 7 4

West
♠ K 7 5 3
♡ 4 2
◇ K J 4
♣ Q J 9 8

East
♠ A 10 9 8
♡ 7
◇ 8 7 6 3
♣ K 10 6 2

South
♠ 2
♡ K Q J 10 8 6 5
◇ A Q 5
♣ 5 3

1.   Partner. If declarer had the ♣ J, he would have won the opening lead with the intention of later leading toward the jack.
2.   The ♣ K.
3.   It is hard to see how it can be wrong to overtake and shitf to a diamond. Partner might be endplayed later in the hand if you do not. You should, in fact, shift to the ◇ 8 to tell you partner you have no interest in the suit.

   Without the diamond shift, declarer can win the second club, ruff a club, draw trumps and lead a spade to the queen and ace. The best you can do is shift — too late — to a diamond which declarer ducks to partner's jack. Partner is now endplayed in three suits.

KEY LESSON POINTERS

1. WHEN PARTNER LEADS THE QUEEN VS. A SUIT CONTRACT AND DUMMY, HOLDING THE ACE PLAYS LOW, THIRD HAND, HOLDING THE KING, KNOWS THAT PARTNER HAS THE JACK AND IS NOT LEADING FROM SHORTNESS. (IF THE LEAD WERE FROM Qx, DECLARER, HOLDING THE JACK WOULD TAKE THE ACE.) IT IS PERFECTLY SAFE FOR THIRD HAND HOLDING K10(x)(x) TO OVERTAKE.
2. LEADING A HIGH SPOT CARD GENERALLY INDICATES WEAKNESS IN THE SUIT. LEADING A LOW SPOT CARD INDICATES THAT THE LEADER CAN STAND A RETURN IN THE SUIT.
3. PARTNER WILL USUALLY BE QUITE IMPRESSED WHEN YOU OVERTAKE ONE OF HIS TRICKS AND HE LATER FINDS OUT THAT IT DIDN'T COST. WHEN YOU FINALLY TELL HIM THAT IT WAS THE ONLY WAY TO DEFEAT THE CONTRACT, HIS ADMIRATION WILL KNOW NO BOUNDS.

(41) WHICH ONE?

Neither side vulnerable
Dealer East

North
♠ K 7 4
♡ A Q 8
◇ 7 4 2
♣ Q 8 4 3

West (you)
♠ 10 8 6 2
♡ 7 5 2
◇ 9 3
♣ J 9 6 2

East	South	West	North
1 ◇	1 NT	Pass	3 NT
All Pass			

Opening Lead: ◇ 9

Partner plays the ◇ 8, and declarer wins the ◇ 10. At trick two declarer runs the ♡ J to partner's king. Partner continues with the ◇ A, felling declarer's queen, and a low diamond to declarer's king, as you pitch a heart.

Declarer plays a heart to dummy, partner playing the ♡ 3, and continues with a third round of hearts, partner following. What do you discard? You remain with four clubs and four spades.

WHICH ONE? (SOLUTION)

North
♠ K 7 4
♡ A Q 8
◇ 7 4 2
♣ Q 8 4 3

<table>
<tr><td>West</td><td>East</td></tr>
<tr><td>♠ 10 8 6 2</td><td>♠ J 3</td></tr>
<tr><td>♡ 7 5 2</td><td>♡ K 9 6 3</td></tr>
<tr><td>◇ 9 3</td><td>◇ A J 8 6 5</td></tr>
<tr><td>♣ J 9 6 2</td><td>♣ K 10</td></tr>
</table>

South
♠ A Q 9 5
♡ J 10 4
◇ K Q 10
♣ A 7 5

You should discard a club for several reasons. (1) Your partner played a low diamond on the third round of the suit indicating strength in the lower ranking suit. If he had spade strength, he would have continued with the ◇ J.

(2) A club discard can only be dangerous if declarer has both the ace and king. Even if he has those cards, he will still need the ♠ A to make his contract. If he has the ♠ A and the ♣ A K, you cannot beat the contract.

A spade discard is far more dangerous. If partner has the jack or queen doubleton of spades, your discard will give declarer four tricks in the suit. If he has the ♣ A to go along with these four spade tricks, he will make the contract. Discard a club.

KEY LESSON POINTERS

1. WHEN FACED WITH A CHOICE OF DISCARDS FROM TWO SUITS, THE GENERAL RULE IS TO KEEP LENGTH PARITY WITH THE DUMMY. HOWEVER, THERE ARE EXCEPTIONS TO EVERY RULE.
2. IF A DISCARD FROM DUMMY'S LENGTH WILL NOT GIVE AWAY THE CONTRACT, THEN YOU MUST CONSIDER MAKING THAT DISCARD, ALTHOUGH IT MAY GIVE UP A TRICK. HERE IT DOES NOT.
3. WHEN PARTNER CLEARS HIS OWN SUIT AT NOTRUMP, ESTABLISHING SMALL CARDS, HE WILL NORMALLY GIVE A SUIT PREFERENCE SIGNAL IF HE HAS A CHOICE OF CARDS WITH WHICH TO CLEAR THE SUIT.
4. PARTNER'S PLAY OF THE ♡ 3 WAS A COUNT SIGNAL INDICATING FOUR HEARTS. ONCE DECLARER IS KNOWN TO HAVE THREE HEARTS AND THREE DIAMONDS, HE MUST HAVE SOME FOUR CARD SUIT. IF THAT SUIT IS SPADES, IT MAY BE DANGEROUS TO DISCARD FROM THAT SUIT.
5. ONCE AGAIN THE ANSWER TO MOST DEFENSIVE PLAYS IS TO COUNT DECLARER'S TRICKS. A CLUB DISCARD CANNOT GIVE HIM NINE, A SPADE DISCARD CAN.

(42) CLEVERNESS (1)

Neither side vulnerable
Dealer South

>   **North**
>   ♠ 9 7 3 2
>   ♡ J 2
>   ◇ A Q 8 7 6 5
>   ♣ A

West (you)
♠ K Q J
♡ K 5 4 3
◇ K 9 2
♣ 4 3 2

South	West	North	East
1 ♡	Pass	2 ◇	Pass
2 ♡	Pass	3 ♡	Pass
4 ♡	All Pass		

Opening Lead: ♠ K

You continue with a second and third spade, declarer ruffing the third round with the ♡ 6.

Declarer cashes the ♣ A, partner playing the ♣ 8, and runs the ♡ J, partner playing the ♡ 8, declarer the ♡ 7.

1. Do you win this trick? If so, what do you return?

Don't worry about your return, you are not winning this trick.

2. A second heart is played from dummy. Partner plays the ♡ 9 and declarer the ♡ Q.

What is declarer's distribution, and what do you do now?

CLEVERNESS (SOLUTION)

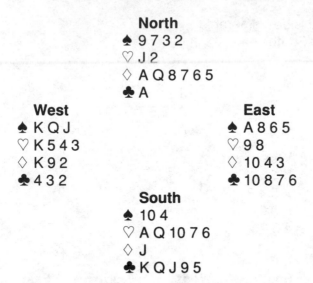

North
♠ 9 7 3 2
♡ J 2
◇ A Q 8 7 6 5
♣ A

West
♠ K Q J
♡ K 5 4 3
◇ K 9 2
♣ 4 3 2

East
♠ A 8 6 5
♡ 9 8
◇ 10 4 3
♣ 10 8 7 6

South
♠ 10 4
♡ A Q 10 7 6
◇ J
♣ K Q J 9 5

2.   Declarer is marked with 2-5-1-5 from the bidding, the fall of the cards, and partner's count signal in clubs showing an even number.

You should win the ♡ K and return the ◇ K, the only card in your hand that defeats the contract. Declarer is now locked in dummy and cannot get off without ruffing either a diamond or a spade. Once he does that, your fourth trump promotes.

KEY LESSON POINTERS

1. WHEN YOU HOLD Kxxx IN THE TRUMP SUIT BEHIND DECLARER, IT IS GENERALLY GOOD TECHNIQUE TO REFUSE THE FIRST FINESSE AND WIN THE SECOND. THIS PLAY REAPS HUGE REWARDS WHEN DUMMY HAS A DOUBLETON TRUMP MAKING IT DIFFICULT FOR DECLARER TO RETURN TO HIS HAND TO DRAW THE REMAINING TRUMPS.

2. WHEN YOU ARE GIVING A COUNT SIGNAL, YOU SHOULD PLAY SECOND HIGH FROM FOUR UNLESS THE FOUR CARDS ARE SEQUENTIAL AND HEADED BY AN HONOR. IN THAT CASE PLAY THE HIGHEST. WITH 10876 SIGNAL COUNT WITH THE EIGHT. WITH 109 OR J10 COMBINATIONS, SIGNAL WITH THE HIGHER HONOR IF YOU CAN AFFORD IT. FROM 10986 SIGNAL COUNT WITH THE 10, BUT WITH 10954 THE BEST YOU USUALLY CAN DO IS THE FIVE.

(43) TRIPLE JUMP RAISE

Both sides vulnerable
Dealer West

North
♠ 5 4 3 2
♡ K 10 7 6
◇ 6 2
♣ Q 9 3

West (you)
♠ K 10 9 6
♡ 4 2
◇ K Q J 10 3
♣ K 8

West	North	East	South
1 ◇	Pass	4 ◇	4 ♡
All Pass	Pass		

Opening Lead: ◇ K

East overtakes and returns the ♠ J. Declarer wins the ♠ A and plunks down the ♣ A.

Do you play the ♣ 8 or the ♣ K? Careful, this could be a trick question.

TRIPLE JUMP RAISE (SOLUTION)

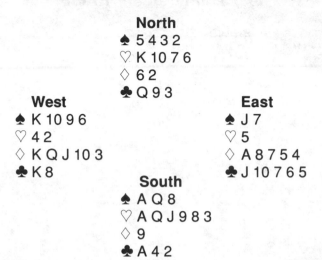

North
♠ 5 4 3 2
♡ K 10 7 6
♢ 6 2
♣ Q 9 3

West
♠ K 10 9 6
♡ 4 2
♢ K Q J 10 3
♣ K 8

East
♠ J 7
♡ 5
♢ A 8 7 5 4
♣ J 10 7 6 5

South
♠ A Q 8
♡ A Q J 9 8 3
♢ 9
♣ A 4 2

You should unblock the ♣ K, and this is not a trick question. Would I do that to you?

In order to defeat this contract you are going to have to take two spades and a club. If you play low on the club, it isn't hard to visualize what will happen. Declarer will draw trumps, ruff a diamond and exit a club.

You will be stuck on lead with the ♣ K and forced to lead either a diamond which will be a ruff and a sluff, or a spade, giving South his tenth trick with the ♠ Q.

You must hope that declarer's distribution is 3-6-1-3 rather than 4-6-1-2. You cannot defeat the contract if he has the latter distribution whether or not you unblock in clubs. If you unblock, a spade can be ducked into you after the hand is stripped. If you don't unblock you will be thrown in with a club after the red suits are stripped.

KEY LESSON POINTERS

1. ALWAYS ASK YOURSELF WHERE YOUR DEFENSIVE TRICKS ARE COMING FROM.
2. BE CAREFUL ABOUT PLAYING LOW AUTOMATICALLY FROM Kx WHEN THE ACE IS PLUNKED DOWN. IT IS POSSIBLE DECLARER IS SETTING UP A STRIP AND IS HOPING TO THROW YOU IN AT A CONVENIENT (FOR HIM) MOMENT. IF YOU CAN FORESEE THAT YOU MAY NOT, OR WILL NOT, HAVE A SAFE EXIT, UN-BLOCK THE KING. YOUR PARTNER WILL BE VERY IMPRESSED.
3. A TRIPLE JUMP RAISE IN A MINOR GUARANTEES A MINIMUM OF FIVE CARD SUPPORT. THE PLAYER MAKING THE RAISE WILL USUALLY HAVE A TOTAL OF TEN CARDS IN THE MINORS. (HE IS NOT APT TO BYPASS A MAJOR SUIT TO RAISE A MINOR.) WITH 11 MINOR SUIT CARDS HE WILL USUALLY JUMP TO GAME IN THE MINOR. KNOWING THAT ALLOWS YOU TO COUNT THE HAND A BIT MORE EASILY. FOR EXAMPLE, WHEN SOUTH FOLLOWED TO THE FIRST DIA-MOND IT INDICATED THAT EAST HAD RAISED WITH A FIVE CARD HOLDING. WITH SIX CLUBS AND FIVE DIAMONDS HE WOULD HAVE JUMPED TO FIVE DIA-MONDS, THEREFORE EAST HAS THREE MAJOR SUIT CARDS. WHAT CAN THEY BE? EITHER TWO SPADES AND ONE HEART OR ONE SPADE AND TWO HEARTS. IF EAST HAS ONE SPADE AND TWO HEARTS, SOUTH WOULD HAVE STARTED WITH 4-5-1-3 DISTRIBUTION AND WOULD HAVE DOUBLED 4 ♢. THEREFORE, EAST HAS TWO SPADES AND ONE HEART AND YOU CAN DEFEAT THE CON-TRACT IF PARTNER HAS THE ♣ J. DO YOU REMEMBER WHEN BRIDGE WAS FUN?

(44) A LITTLE LEARNING

East-West vulnerable
Dealer South

North
♠ 3 2
♡ K Q 7 5
◇ A 10 7 5
♣ 9 5 4

East (you)
♠ J 10 8
♡ A J 10 8
◇ K 3
♣ Q 10 8 6

South	West	North	East
1 ♠	Pass	1 NT	Pass
4 ♠	All Pass		

Opening Lead: ◇ 2   (Third or fifth best)

Dummy plays low, you win the ◇ K and declarer plays the ◇ Q. What do you return at trick two?

A LITTLE LEARNING (SOLUTION)

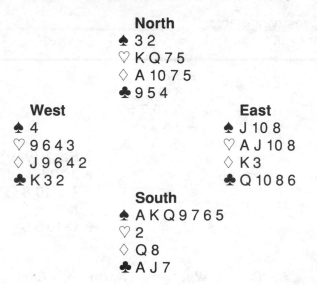

North
- ♠ 3 2
- ♡ K Q 7 5
- ◇ A 10 7 5
- ♣ 9 5 4

West
- ♠ 4
- ♡ 9 6 4 3
- ◇ J 9 6 4 2
- ♣ K 3 2

East
- ♠ J 10 8
- ♡ A J 10 8
- ◇ K 3
- ♣ Q 10 8 6

South
- ♠ A K Q 9 7 6 5
- ♡ 2
- ◇ Q 8
- ♣ A J 7

Return a diamond and kill the dummy while you still remain with trumps.

Declarer figures to have seven solid spades, and the lead has indicated that declarer has a doubleton diamond.

Your club winners cannot disappear if you return a diamond. You will get them later. However, if you return a club (the ten indicates you've been reading your bridge books), you will soon see one of your club tricks go away on the ◇ A. Declarer will win the ♣ A, draw trumps, finesse the ◇ 10 and discard a club on the ◇ A.

KEY LESSON POINTERS

1. THE DIFFERENCE BETWEEN AN AVERAGE AND AN EXPERT DEFENDER IS THE ABILITY TO KNOW WHEN TRICKS CAN GET AWAY AND WHEN THEY CAN'T. WHEN TRICKS CAN GET AWAY, AN ACTIVE DEFENSE IS CALLED FOR; WHEN THEY CANNOT, A PASSIVE DEFENSE IS IN ORDER.

2. IF A DEFENDER CAN "KILL THE DUMMY", HE CAN, WITH ONE STROKE, TURN AN ACTIVE DEFENSE INTO A PASSIVE ONE. IN THIS CASE, A DIAMOND RETURN KILLS THE DUMMY.

3. THIRD AND FIFTH BEST LEADS VS. SUIT CONTRACTS MAKE IT EASIER TO READ THE LEAD WHEN THE LOWEST CARD IS LED. IT WILL BE FROM EITHER A THREE OR A FIVE CARD SUIT, AS OPPOSED TO A THREE OR A FOUR CARD SUIT WHEN LEADING FOURTH BEST. WHEN THE NINE IS IN THE DUMMY BEGIN WITH THE ♣ 10. GIVEN THAT DECLARER HAS NO DISCARDS AVAILABLE IN ANY SIDE SUIT, THE LEAD OF THE ♣ 10 LIMITS DECLARER TO ONE TRICK. THE LEAD OF A LOW CLUB GIVES DECLARER TWO TRICKS IF HE DUCKS THE LEAD AROUND TO THE NINE AND LATER FINESSES THE JACK.

A SIMILAR, BUT NOT AS WELL KNOWN "SURROUNDING PLAY" IS:

North
♠ K 8 2

West
♠ J 5 4

East
♠ Q 9 7 3

South
♠ A 10 6

IF EAST ATTACKS SPADES, HE MUST ATTACK WITH THE ♠ 9 TO INSURE A TRICK IN THE SUIT.

(45) EVERYTHING UNDER CONTROL

East-West vulnerable
Dealer South

North
♠ Q 7 6 3 2
♡ K 9 8 7
◇ 10 5 4
♣ 10

West (you)
♠ A J 10 9 4
♡ 10
◇ A Q 9
♣ J 9 8 7

South	West	North	East
1 ♡	1 ♠	3 ♡*	Pass
4 ♡	All Pass		

*Preemptive in competition

Opening Lead: ♣ 7

Partner plays the ♣ Q and declarer wins the ♣ A. Declarer plays the ♡ K and ♡ A; partner follows with a low heart and then the queen, as you discard a spade.

Declarer continues with the ♣ K, discarding a diamond from dummy, and ruffs the ♣ 2, partner playing the ♣ 6 and ♣ 5.

With the lead in dummy, declarer leads a low diamond to his king, partner playing the ◇ 2. After you win the ◇ A, what do you play?

EVERYTHING UNDER CONTROL (SOLUTION)

North
- ♠ Q 7 6 3 2
- ♡ K 9 8 7
- ◇ 10 5 4
- ♣ 10

West
- ♠ A J 10 9 4
- ♡ 10
- ◇ A Q 9
- ♣ J 9 8 7

East
- ♠ K
- ♡ Q 4
- ◇ J 8 7 6 2
- ♣ Q 6 5 4 3

South
- ♠ 8 5
- ♡ A J 6 5 3 2
- ◇ K 3
- ♣ A K 2

You must return a low spade — if you are counting! Declarer is known to have six hearts, once partner's queen appears, and either three or five clubs, judging from partner's present count signal in that suit.

As the hand cannot be beaten if declarer has five clubs, and as the play would not be going this way if he had, assume declarer has three clubs.

When partner plays the ◇ 2 at trick six, also a count signal, the picture is complete. Declarer started with 2-6-2-3. The only chance to defeat this contract is to win a total of four tricks in spades and diamonds — two in each suit. In order to do that, partner must have the blank king of spades, and the suit must be led now before the hand is stripped.

After partner wins the ♠ K, he leads a diamond to your queen, and you cash the ♠ A for the setting trick. A symphony.

KEY LESSON POINTERS

1. PARTNER IS SUPPOSED TO HELP YOU WITH THE COUNT, PARTICULARLY WHEN HE HAS A WEAK HAND.
2. TAKE EACH SUIT IN TURN. WHEN PARTNER PLAYS THE ♡ Q HE DENIES THE ♡ J, SO YOU KNOW HE HAS NO MORE TRUMPS.

   IN CLUBS, PARTNER IS SUPPOSED TO GIVE PRESENT COUNT AFTER HAVING PLAYED THIRD HAND HIGH TO THE FIRST TRICK. PRESENT COUNT MEANS PLAYING THE LOWEST REMAINING CARD WHEN AN ODD NUMBER OF CARDS REMAINS AND THE HIGHEST CARD YOU CAN AFFORD WHEN AN EVEN NUMBER OF CARDS REMAINS. HAD EAST STARTED WITH EITHER ♣ Q 6 4 3, OR ♣ Q 7 6 5 4 3, HIS PROPER PLAY THE SECOND TIME THE SUIT IS LED IS THE ♣ 3.

   IN DIAMONDS, PARTNER ALSO GIVES THE COUNT SIGNAL — LOW FROM ODD, USUALLY SECOND HIGH FROM FOUR, AND TOP OF A DOUBLETON.

   PUTTING ALL OF THIS INFORMATION TOGETHER FINALLY ALLOWS YOU TO COUNT DECLARER'S HAND AND MAKE THE WINNING PLAY. MAZELTOV.

(46) EARLY PLAY

Neither side vulnerable
Dealer South

North
♠ 9 6 4 2
♡ A 10 4
◇ A 5 3
♣ 10 5 4

East (you)
♠ 7
♡ K 9 6 5
◇ 9 8 7 2
♣ K 8 7 2

South	West	North	East
1 ♠	Dbl.	2 ♠	3 ♡
3 ♠	All Pass		

Opening Lead: ◇ Q

Declarer wins in dummy and leads a low heart. Which heart do you play?

EARLY PLAY (SOLUTION)

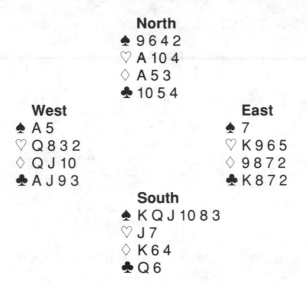

North
♠ 9 6 4 2
♡ A 10 4
◇ A 5 3
♣ 10 5 4

West
♠ A 5
♡ Q 8 3 2
◇ Q J 10
♣ A J 9 3

East
♠ 7
♡ K 9 6 5
◇ 9 8 7 2
♣ K 8 7 2

South
♠ K Q J 10 8 3
♡ J 7
◇ K 6 4
♣ Q 6

Play low. Early leads from an ace are among the most difficult that second hand has to face. Sometimes you may be ducking the setting trick!

There are no 100% rules, but here are a few that might help you decide whether to take the trick or duck in second seat.

1.   If it is the setting trick, and there is the least possibility that it might go away, take it.
2.   If it is important that you be on lead, and this is your last chance to be on lead, take the trick.
3.   If declarer has slow losers (losers that you cannot grab immediately), duck the trick.
4.   If declarer is clearly trying to set up this suit for a discard, consider declarer's possible holdings in view of the bidding. In this case if declarer has Qx you can do nothing, as declarer can unblock the queen if you win the king and later finesse the 10. However, if declarer has Jx you are being taken for a swindle. By rising you give declarer two tricks (after the unblock) instead of the one that he was entitled to.

KEY LESSON POINTERS

1.   TRY TO PREPARE YOURSELF FOR THE PLAYS YOU LEAST WANT TO SEE. FOR EXAMPLE, YOU SHOULD ASK YOURSELF — WHAT WILL I DO IF DECLARER LEADS A LOW HEART FROM DUMMY? — BEFORE HE MAKES THE PLAY.
2.   DUCKING IN THE TRUMP SUIT IS A MUCH EASIER PLAY. IF DECLARER HAD ALL OF THE TOP HONORS SAVE THE KING, HE WOULD BE FINESSING THE OTHER WAY. THE VERY FACT THAT HE IS LEADING LOW FROM THE ACE INDICATES HE IS MISSING ONE OR, MORE LIKELY, TWO HONORS.

North
♠ A 6 5

West
♠ Q 8

East (you)
♠ K 9 4

South
♠ J 10 7 3 2

SPADES ARE TRUMP AND A LOW SPADE IS LED FROM DUMMY. IT IS USUALLY RIGHT FOR SECOND HAND TO PLAY LOW (QUICKLY) IN THESE SITUATIONS. PARTNER IS VERY APT TO HAVE THE JACK, THE QUEEN, OR BOTH!

(47) WILL I LOOK BAD?

North-South vulnerable
Dealer East

North
♠ A K Q J
♡ A K Q 9
◇ –
♣ A Q 7 6 5

East (you)
♠ 4
♡ J 3 2
◇ K J 10 9 6 5
♣ K 10 2

East	South	West	North
2 ◇*	Pass	3 ◇	4 ◇
Pass	4 ♡	Pass	5 ◇
Pass	5 ♡	Pass	6 ♡
All Pass			
*Weak			

Opening Lead: ◇ 2

Dummy ruffs the opening lead and a low club is led from dummy. It's your turn.

WILL I LOOK BAD? (SOLUTION)

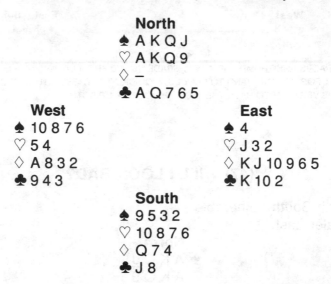

North
♠ A K Q J
♡ A K Q 9
◇ –
♣ A Q 7 6 5

West
♠ 10 8 7 6
♡ 5 4
◇ A 8 3 2
♣ 9 4 3

East
♠ 4
♡ J 3 2
◇ K J 10 9 6 5
♣ K 10 2

South
♠ 9 5 3 2
♡ 10 8 7 6
◇ Q 7 4
♣ J 8

Rise with the king and return a diamond. There are many more reasons to win this trick than to duck it.

First, where is the ◇ A? If partner has that card, which seems likely, you have an automatic set by winning and returning a diamond. Once dummy ruffs with a trump honor, your ♡ J becomes the setting trick.

If declarer has the ◇ A, why didn't he win the trick in his hand and take the club finesse through the partner of the weak two bidder, the player who usually has the missing outside honors?

Can it ever be right to duck the club? Yes. If declarer has xxx 10xxx Axx xxx you must play low in order to defeat the slam.

In fact, you should always cite this hand as an example of why you played low if the opponents wind up making the slam. The post-mortem figures to be quite lively.

KEY LESSON POINTERS

1. WHEN DUMMY IS MARKED WITH A VOID, IT IS NOT UNUSUAL FOR A DEFENDER TO UNDERLEAD AN ACE IN THE VOID SUIT ON OPENING LEAD. ALLOW FOR IT.

2. LEADING LOW AWAY FROM AN AQ COMBINATION GENERALLY MEANS THAT DECLARER HAS ENTRY PROBLEMS — OR HAS THREE SMALL AND IS PLANNING TO FINESSE THE QUEEN NEXT TIME AROUND.

3. IF DECLARER HAS THE ◇ A, PARTNER HAS AN EXTREMELY WEAK HAND WITH NOTHING OTHER THAN THE ◇ Q. HE MIGHT HAVE SAVED AT 7 ◇ AT THE PREVAILING VULNERABILITY WITH THAT HAND. (BEFORE THE NEW SCORING CHANGE). NOW DOUBLED UNDERTRICKS NOT VULNERABLE ARE 100, 300, 500, 800, 1100, 1400, etc. INSTEAD OF 100, 300, 500, 700, 900, 1100, etc.

(48) SUPER SLEUTH

Neither side vulnerable
Dealer West

North
♠ A J 10 4
♡ A 10 2
◊ 7 2
♣ A K Q 9

West (you)
♠ 8 3
♡ K J 7
◊ K Q 10 5
♣ J 8 4 3

West	North	East	South
Pass	1 ♣	Pass	1 ♠
Pass	3 ♠	Pass	4 ◊
Pass	4 ♡	Pass	6 ♠
All Pass			

Opening Lead: ◊ K

Declarer wins the ◊ A, crosses to dummy with the ♠ A and ruffs a diamond. He crosses to the ♠ J, partner discarding a diamond, and plays three top clubs, discarding three hearts, and ruffs a club in the closed hand.

Declarer then leads a low heart toward dummy.

1. What is declarer's distribution?
2. Which heart do you play? Why?

SUPER SLEUTH (SOLUTION)

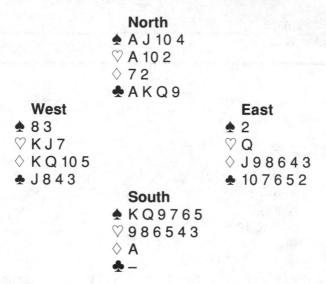

North
♠ A J 10 4
♡ A 10 2
◇ 7 2
♣ A K Q 9

West
♠ 8 3
♡ K J 7
◇ K Q 10 5
♣ J 8 4 3

East
♠ 2
♡ Q
◇ J 9 8 6 4 3
♣ 10 7 6 5 2

South
♠ K Q 9 7 6 5
♡ 9 8 6 5 4 3
◇ A
♣ —

1. Declarer is known to be 6-6-1-0.
2. You must play the ♡ K! This play in itself does not defeat the contract, but it gives you your only chance.

   You must assume your partner has the singleton queen of hearts or else there is nothing you can do. If declarer has the ♡ Q, he has a 100% play of putting in the ♡ 10 if you play low. If you play either honor, he simply loses one heart trick.

   In fact, with his actual holding, he is also planning to put in the ♡ 10. He will win if hearts are 2-2, or if he loses to a singleton honor. East will have to concede a ruff and a sluff.

   By playing the ♡ K, you give declarer food for thought. If your ♡ K is a singleton, he must duck in order to make the hand. If he wins and plays another heart, partner will score two heart tricks with his presumed QJ7.

   Once declarer ducks the ♡ K you are in business. When you return the ♡ 7 he now has to decide who has the ♡ J. Did you play the ♡ K from K7 or KJ7? Anyway, you did the very best you could and get an A for effort.

KEY LESSON POINTERS

1. MOST HIGH LEVEL DEFENSIVE PLAYS COME FROM COUNTING DECLARER'S HAND. THIS ONE COUNTS OUT PERFECTLY.
2. WHEN YOU KNOW THAT THE EXISTING LIE OF THE CARDS WILL ALLOW DECLARER TO MAKE HIS CONTRACT WITH NORMAL PLAYS, YOU MUST DO EVERYTHING IN YOUR POWER TO MAKE HIM BELIEVE THE CARDS LIE OTHERWISE.
3. PUT YOURSELF IN THE DECLARER'S SHOES WHEN YOU ARE DEFENDING. IF YOU CAN FIGURE OUT WHAT HE MUST FEAR, YOU CAN PLAY ON THOSE FEARS — EVEN THOUGH THEY MAY BE NON-EXISTENT.

(49) READY-MADE LEAD

Neither side vulnerable
Dealer North

                    North
                    ♠ 9 4 2
                    ♡ Q J 9
                    ♢ K J
                    ♣ A J 9 7 6

West (you)
♠ A Q 7
♡ K 6 2
♢ 10 9 8 6
♣ 4 3 2

North	East	South	West
1 ♣	Pass	2 NT	Pass
3 NT	All Pass		

Opening Lead: ♢ 10

Dummy plays the jack, partner the queen, and declarer the ace. At trick two declarer leads the ♣ 5 to the ♣ A, partner playing the ♣ 8, and runs the ♡ Q, partner playing the ♡ 5, declarer the ♡ 8.

Do you take the trick? If so, what do you return? If not, why not?

READY-MADE LEAD (SOLUTION)

North
♠ 9 4 2
♡ Q J 9
◇ K J
♣ A J 9 7 6

West
♠ A Q 7
♡ K 6 2
◇ 10 9 8 6
♣ 4 3 2

East
♠ K 6 5 3
♡ 7 5 4 3
◇ Q 7 5 4
♣ 8

South
♠ J 10 8
♡ A 10 8
◇ A 3 2
♣ K Q 10 5

You should win the trick and shift to a spade honor. The fact that declarer is attacking hearts rather than clubs indicates that the clubs are solid. If that is so, declarer has at least nine tricks ready to go: five clubs, two hearts and two diamonds. There is no "time" to set up your diamonds, you must cash out — now!

KEY LESSON POINTERS

1. MOST PLAYERS WILL NOT BYPASS A FOUR CARD MAJOR TO RESPOND 2NT TO AN OPENING MINOR SUIT BID. BE AWARE OF YOUR OPPONENTS' TENDENCIES IN THAT REGARD.
2. IF DECLARER HAS, IN FACT, ONLY THREE HEARTS, ISN'T IT STRANGE THAT HE IS ATTACKING HEARTS AND NOT CLUBS? WHY? BECAUSE THE CLUBS ARE ALREADY GOOD. IF SO, YOU CAN COUNT NINE TRICKS AND MUST SHIFT TO A SPADE.
3. WHEN DECLARER ATTACKS A SHORT SUIT, APPARENTLY STRANDING A LONGER ONE, THE USUAL REASON IS THAT THE LONGER SUIT IS READY TO RUN.
4. LEADING FROM AN AQ CAN BE VERY PLEASANT WHEN PARTNER HAS THE KING. IF DECLARER HAS NINE TRICKS IN THE OTHER THREE SUITS, YOU MIGHT AS WELL GO FOR IT. HOWEVER, BE PREPARED FOR A GRUESOME POST-MORTEM IF DECLARER HAS THE KING.

(50) THIRD SEAT WEAK TWO (1)

Neither side vulnerable
Dealer East

North
♠ A 7 3
♡ A K 10 3 2
◇ Q 7 4
♣ A J

East (You)
♠ K 6 2
♡ 5
◇ J 8 6
♣ Q 10 7 6 3 2

East	South	West	North
Pass	Pass	2 ♠*	Dbl.
3 ♠	4 ♡	All Pass	

*Weak

Opening Lead: ♠ Q

Partner's queen wins the opening and he continues the suit to dummy's ace. At trick three declarer ruffs a spade and then plays the ♡ Q and low to the ♡ A, partner following up the line as you discard a club.

Declarer continues with the ♣ A from dummy, partner playing the ♣ 4, and follows with the ♣ J.

1. Which club do you play?
   You cover with the queen and you win the trick, both declarer and partner playing low.

2. What is declarer's distribution, and what do you play next?

THIRD SEAT WEAK TWO (SOLUTION)

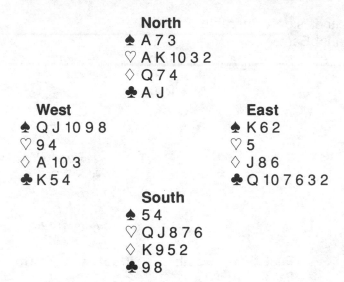

North
♠ A 7 3
♡ A K 10 3 2
◇ Q 7 4
♣ A J

West
♠ Q J 10 9 8
♡ 9 4
◇ A 10 3
♣ K 5 4

East
♠ K 6 2
♡ 5
◇ J 8 6
♣ Q 10 7 6 3 2

South
♠ 5 4
♡ Q J 8 7 6
◇ K 9 5 2
♣ 9 8

2.   Declarer's hand is an open book. His original distribution was 2-5-4-2.

At this point you have to work out a way to get two diamond tricks, assuming partner has at least the ace.

If declarer has K109x, there is no defense. If declarer has K10xx, you are also in bad shape unless you are playing against a very imaginative declarer. If, when you lead a diamond, he decides your partner has the AJ9, he can make the hand if he rises with the ◇ K.

However, you have a legitimate way to defeat the contract if declarer has K9xx. Lead the ◇ 8. Given the layout of the suit, this is the <u>only</u> card in your hand that insures taking two diamond tricks. The best declarer can do is cover with the nine, but when partner plays the ten, declarer's goose is cooked.

KEY LESSON POINTERS

1. WHEN A HAND REDUCES TO A ONE SUIT ENDING, DEFENDERS MUST ALWAYS ASK THEMSELVES THE SAME FOUR QUESTIONS WHEN THROWN IN.
   (a) WHO SHOULD BE TAKING THE TRICK? (ASSUMING THERE IS A CHOICE)
   (b) HOW MANY TRICKS DO WE NEED FROM THE SUIT?
   (c) WHAT IS THE MINIMUM HOLDING I MUST FIND IN MY PARTNER'S HAND TO GET   THE DESIRED NUMBER OF TRICKS?
   (d) GIVEN THAT HE HAS THIS HOLDING, WHAT IS THE BEST CARD FOR ME T0 ATTACK WITH?
2. IN THE ACTUAL LAYOUT, IF YOU ATTACK WITH THE ◇ J, YOU WILL PROBABLY DEFEAT THE HAND ALSO. IF DECLARER PLAYS LOW, HE MUST LOSE TWO TRICKS. HOWEVER, IF HE PLAYS THE KING, HE LOSES ONLY ONE. ALSO, YOU LOSE THE SWINDLE POSSIBILITIES IF DECLARER HAS K10xx AND HAS DECIDED TO PLAY YOUR PARTNER FOR THE AJ IF YOU LEAD LOW.
3. ALLOW FOR A FIVE CARD SUIT WHEN PARTNER OPENS A WEAK TWO IN THIRD SEAT.

Section IV
PLAY

BACK COVER HAND - TO MAKE A DISCARD (SOLUTION)

North
♠ A K Q
♡ A K Q J 2
◇ A
♣ A K Q 2

West
♠ 10 9 8 7
♡ 3
◇ 4 3 2
♣ 8 7 6 5 4

East
♠ 6 5
♡ 10 9 8 7 6 5
◇ Q 10 9
♣ J 10

South
♠ J 4 3 2
♡ 4
◇ K J 8 7 6 5
♣ 9 3

Believe it or not, unless you throw a diamond, declarer makes the hand!

You can see 11 top tricks staring you in the face, and if declarer has ♣ 9xx he can always make four club tricks so you must assume that declarer has either two or three small clubs. However, if he has ♣ 9x and the ◇ K, a club discard will allow him to get to his hand with the ♣ 9 and make an overtrick!

There is no reason for you to save diamonds. Declarer has no way back to his hand to cash the ◇ K, and if he does, he will take all 13 tricks regardless. Why not a heart?

If you discard a heart, declarer can cash dummy's eleven top tricks and throw you in with a heart. You will now have to concede the last trick to declarer's king of diamonds.

But if your last two cards are hearts and partner's last two cards are clubs, declarer must go down one.

(26) PARTSCORE DOGFIGHT (1) (2)

Neither side vulnerable
Dealer West

North
♠ Q 7 6 5
♡ J 8 7
◇ K 10 9
♣ A 7 4

South
♠ A J 10 9 8
♡ A 2
◇ 8 7 6 5
♣ J 10

West	North	East	South
1 ♡	Pass	Pass	1 ♠
2 ♣	2 ♠	3 ♡	3 ♠
All Pass			

Opening Lead: ♡ 5

1. How do you read the heart position, and which heart do you play from dummy?
    East must have one of the high heart honors or else West would have led the ♡ K. As there is no point in playing the ♡ J, you should play low.
2. You play low from dummy and East plays the ♡ 9. Do you take the trick or not?
    Although it probably doesn't matter, it is better to duck the trick to break up East-West communications.
3. East returns a low heart to your ace and West's three. Now you are on your own. How do you continue?

PARTSCORE DOGFIGHT (SOLUTION)

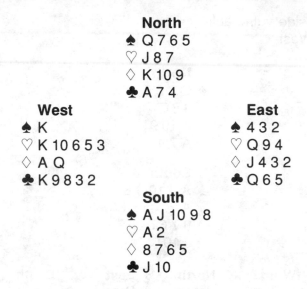

North
♠ Q 7 6 5
♡ J 8 7
♢ K 10 9
♣ A 7 4

West
♠ K
♡ K 10 6 5 3
♢ A Q
♣ K 9 8 3 2

East
♠ 4 3 2
♡ Q 9 4
♢ J 4 3 2
♣ Q 6 5

South
♠ A J 10 9 8
♡ A 2
♢ 8 7 6 5
♣ J 10

3.   East is marked with a heart honor, probably a club honor (West didn't lead the ♣ K) and surely has at least the ♢ J (if West had 1-5-3-4 distribution he would have doubled 1 ♠). Therefore West must have the ♠ K, otherwise East would have been able to respond to the opening 1 ♡ bid. Although it is safe to fool around with this hand a bit (duck a club, for example, with the intention of perhaps stripping the hand and playing ace and a spade), the main idea is <u>not</u> to take the spade finesse.

KEY LESSON POINTERS

1.   WHEN YOU HAVE Jxx IN THE DUMMY FACING Ax IN YOUR HAND, PLAY LOW FROM THE DUMMY WHEN THE SUIT IS LED VS. A TRUMP CONTRACT. THIRD HAND VERY LIIKELY HAS Q9x, K9x, Q9xx OR K9xx. IF THIRD HAND ERRS AND DOES NOT PLAY THE NINE YOU GAIN A TRICK.
2.   GIVEN THE SPADE POSITION ON THIS HAND, THE NORMAL PLAY, OF COURSE, IS TO FINESSE. HOWEVER, HERE THE BIDDING HAS TOLD YOU THAT THE FINESSE WON'T WORK, SO YOU MIGHT AS WELL HOPE THE KING IS SINGLETON. AS AN ADDITIONAL PRECAUTION YOU MIGHT TRY LEADING THE ♠ Q FROM DUMMY. EVEN THOUGH YOU ARE GOING TO PLAY THE ACE, EVERY SO OFTEN YOUR CALCULATIONS GO ASTRAY AND YOU GET AN UNEXPECTED COVER.
3.   WHEN IT CAN'T HURT TO LEAD AN HONOR FROM ONE HAND TOWARD THE OTHER, DO IT!

(27) SMALL LEAP (1) (2)

North-South vulnerable
Dealer East

North
♠ A 9 6 4
♡ –
◇ K J 9 8
♣ K J 4 3 2

South
♠ 7
♡ A Q 8 7 4 2
◇ A Q 7 6
♣ A 5

East	South	West	North
2 ♠*	3 ♡	Pass	3 ♠
Pass	4 ◇	Pass	6 ◇
*Weak			

Opening Lead: ♠ 5

1. You win the ♠ A in dummy. What do you play at trick two?
    You ruff a spade low; West follows with the ♠ 2.
2. How do you continue?
    You play the ♡ A, discarding a spade, and ruff a heart low in dummy — all following.
3. Now what?

SMALL LEAP (SOLUTION)

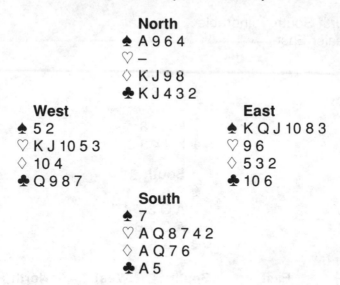

North
♠ A 9 6 4
♡ –
♢ K J 9 8
♣ K J 4 3 2

West
♠ 5 2
♡ K J 10 5 3
♢ 10 4
♣ Q 9 8 7

East
♠ K Q J 10 8 3
♡ 9 6
♢ 5 3 2
♣ 10 6

South
♠ 7
♡ A Q 8 7 4 2
♢ A Q 7 6
♣ A 5

3.   Your play is to ruff one more heart low in dummy and one club low in your hand and then crossruff. However, you must be careful to cash both high clubs before ruffing the third heart.

East may have a doubleton heart and a doubleton club and will discard a club on the third heart — if he cannot overruff dummy.

Therefore, you should cash the ♣ K and the ♣ A and then ruff a heart low in dummy. Assuming this wins, ruff a club low in your hand and continue with a high crossruff for twelve tricks.

Yes, West, looking at those hearts as well as a potential club stopper, should have led a trump. However, a great player like you would have still made the hand, right?

KEY LESSON POINTERS

1. BEFORE EMBARKING ON A CROSSRUFF, CASH YOUR TOP CARDS IN THE SIDE SUITS BEFORE YOU DO TOO MUCH RUFFING. IF YOU DON'T CASH THEM EARLY, YOU MAY NOT BE ABLE TO CASH THEM LATER!
2. BEFORE EMBARKING ON A CROSSRUFF, COUNT YOUR SURE TRICKS OUTSIDE OF THE TRUMP SUIT TO DETERMINE HOW MANY TRUMP TRICKS YOU NEED. HERE YOU HAVE FOUR SIDE WINNERS SO YOU ARE PLAYING FOR EIGHT TRUMP TRICKS.
3. ENTRY CONSIDERATIONS SOMETIMES PREVENT YOU FROM CASHING ALL YOUR SIDE WINNERS AT ONCE. IN THIS CASE, YOU COULD NOT CASH YOUR CLUBS AT ONCE BECAUSE YOU NEEDED THE ♣ A AS A HAND REENTRY TO RUFF THE THIRD HEART BEFORE RUFFING A CLUB. WITH 6-3-2-2 DISTRIBUTION, EAST CAN DISCARD HIS LAST HEART ON A CLUB RUFF, PUTTING YOU AT RISK WHEN YOU TRUMP A THIRD ROUND OF HEARTS.

(28) A GREAT SLAM (1) (2) (3)

Both sides vulnerable
Dealer South

North
♠ A 4
♡ A Q 2
◇ Q 10 6 5
♣ K J 3 2

South
♠ Q 5
♡ K J 9 8 7
◇ A K 2
♣ A 10 9

South	West	North	East
1 NT	Pass	4 NT	Pass
6 ♡ *	All Pass		

*Five card suit plus maximum

Opening Lead: ♠ 2 (Low from an odd number)

1. Which spade do you play from dummy? Why?
    You rise with the ♠ A because (a) West is unlikely to be underleading the ♠ K vs. a slam into the notrump bidder and (b) you have alternate plays.
2. What are they?
    Your next move should be to draw two rounds of trumps with the AQ and exit a spade. If the player with the ♠ K, probably East, does not have the odd trump, he will be endplayed in three suits.
3. When you concede the spade, East does win the trick; but, alas, he refuses to cooperate and exits with the third trump, West discarding a spade.
    How do you continue?
    Test the diamonds hoping that either the jack drops or the suit divides three-three. Alas again, that unfriendly East persists in thwarting your plans. You discover that he started with ◇Jxxx as West discards another spade on the third diamond.
4. One can only lead you by the hand so far. Now it's your turn. Who has the Queen of clubs?

A GREAT SLAM (SOLUTION)

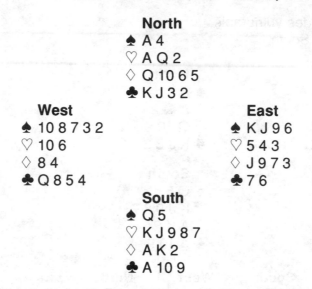

North
- ♠ A 4
- ♡ A Q 2
- ◇ Q 10 6 5
- ♣ K J 3 2

West
- ♠ 10 8 7 3 2
- ♡ 10 6
- ◇ 8 4
- ♣ Q 8 5 4

East
- ♠ K J 9 6
- ♡ 5 4 3
- ◇ J 9 7 3
- ♣ 7 6

South
- ♠ Q 5
- ♡ K J 9 8 7
- ◇ A K 2
- ♣ A 10 9

4.   You should play West for the ♣ Q because West started with four clubs and East only two. West is twice as likely to hold the ♣ Q as East.

This is yet another hand that shows how important it is to count. West should have five spades and has turned up with doubletons in each of the red suits, ergo, four clubs.

KEY LESSON POINTERS

1. ONE SHOULD NOT ASSUME THAT A DEFENDER IS UNDERLEADING A KING VS. A SLAM INTO A NOTRUMP BIDDER WHEN THERE IS NO KNOWN DANGER OF A LONG SIDE SUIT IN DUMMY.

2. SOMETIMES A HAND CAN BE PARTIALLY STRIPPED, SUCH AS THIS ONE. BY LEAVING ONE TRUMP AT LARGE YOU CAN STILL FORCE A RUFF AND A SLUFF OR A FAVORABLE SWITCH IF THE PLAYER BEING THROWN IN DOES NOT HAVE THE ODD TRUMP.

3. THE LEAD OF A LOW CARD FROM AN ODD NUMBER AND THIRD HIGH FROM AN EVEN NUMBER VS. A SUIT CONTRACT IS AN EXTREMELY POPULAR LEAD CONVENTION AND IS USED IN TOURNAMENT PLAY AS OFTEN AS FOURTH BEST. USING THIS METHOD, THE DEUCE IS LED FROM Q72 OR Q7642 AND FIVE IS LED FROM K852 AND K85432. PLAYING HIGH-LOW INDICATES AN EVEN NUMBER OF CARDS. THE BIDDING WILL USUALLY DISTINGUISH BETWEEN TWO CARD LENGTH DIFFERENTIALS. THE MAJOR ADVANTAGE OF THE CONVENTION IS THAT THIRD HAND CAN TELL IMMEDIATELY WHEN THE LOWEST CARD IS LED THAT PARTNER CANNOT HAVE A FOUR CARD SUIT. A MAJOR DISADVANTAGE IS HAVING TO LEAD THE SEVEN OR EIGHT FROM FOUR CARD HOLDINGS SUCH AS Q1072 OR K1083.

4. SIDE SUITS THAT OFFER A TWO-WAY FINESSE FOR A QUEEN ARE ALMOST ALWAYS SAVED UNTIL THE VERY END. NOTICE DECLARER'S TECHNIQUE IN LEAVING THE CLUB SUIT UNTIL THE VERY LAST. HE WAS ABLE TO GET A COMPLETE COUNT ON THE HAND.

(29) ONE SUIT FINALE (1)

Neither side vulnerable
Dealer South

North
♠ K 9 5
♡ K 9
◇ A Q 7 5
♣ J 7 6 2

South
♠ A 10
♡ A J
◇ K J 10 8 6 3
♣ A 10 3

South	West	North	East
1 ◇	Pass	2 NT	Pass
4 NT	Pass	6 ◇	All Pass

Opening Lead: ◇ 2, East follows.

1. What is your general plan?
    You should strip the hand before you attack clubs.
2. How do you attack clubs if you feel that the longer clubs
    are with East? With West?

ONE SUIT FINALE (SOLUTION)

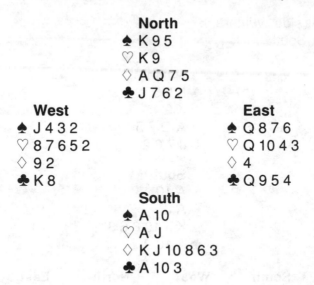

North
♠ K 9 5
♡ K 9
♢ A Q 7 5
♣ J 7 6 2

West
♠ J 4 3 2
♡ 8 7 6 5 2
♢ 9 2
♣ K 8

East
♠ Q 8 7 6
♡ Q 10 4 3
♢ 4
♣ Q 9 5 4

South
♠ A 10
♡ A J
♢ K J 10 8 6 3
♣ A 10 3

2.   If you think East has the club length, lead the ♣ J from dummy after the hand has been stripped. If East plays low, you play low and can lose only one club trick.

If East covers, win the ace, enter dummy with a trump and lead a club to the ten. If it loses to the remaining honor, and that honor is doubleton, you still lose only one trick as West must give you a ruff and a sluff.

If the longer clubs are with West, play East for honor doubleton and lead low to the ten. Assuming this loses and a club comes back, play low from dummy and hope an honor appears from East. The reason you play this way rather than play West for both honors, is that West might have led the king from king-queen fourth had he been dealt that holding.

If you feel clubs are 3-3 you have to hope one player has both honors. However you might lead the ♣ J from dummy and hope East does not cover with Kxx or Qxx. This swindle works better when the dummy has 10xxx and declarer AJx.

KEY LESSON POINTERS

1. WHEN THERE ARE LOSERS IN ONLY ONE SUIT, STRIP THE HAND, IF POSSIBLE, BEFORE YOU ATTACK THE SUIT.
2. IF YOU KNOW WHICH OPPONENT IS LONGER IN THE CRITICAL SUIT IT MAY HELP YOU DECIDE HOW TO ATTACK THE SUIT.
3. Jxxx FACING A10x IS A COMBINATION THAT MUST BE UNDERSTOOD — PARTICULARLY IF DECLARER PLANS TO STRIP THE HAND BEFORE ATTACKING THE SUIT.

(30) MINOR TWO-SUITER (1)

East-West vulnerable
Dealer South

North
♠ A 6 4
♡ A Q 8 7 6
◇ K 5
♣ 10 4 3

South
♠ 3
♡ 9 5
◇ A Q J 9 2
♣ K Q 9 8 7

South	West	North	East
1 ◇	Pass	1 ♡	Pass
2 ♣	Pass	2 ♠	Pass
3 ♣	Pass	3 ◇	Pass
3 ♡	Pass	4 ♣	Pass
5 ♣	All Pass		

Opening Lead: ♠ 2

1.   You win the ♠ A and lead a low club to the king which holds. Now what?
    You cross to dummy with the ◇ K and lead another <u>low</u> club.
2.   When you do that East discards a spade and you duck to West's ♣ J. West continues with a spade which you ruff.
    How do you continue from here?

MINOR TWO-SUITER (SOLUTION)

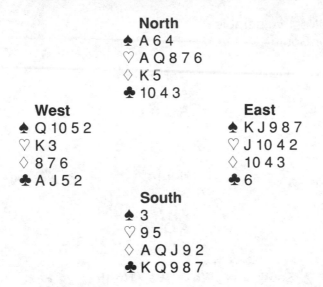

North
♠ A 6 4
♡ A Q 8 7 6
◇ K 5
♣ 10 4 3

West
♠ Q 10 5 2
♡ K 3
◇ 8 7 6
♣ A J 5 2

East
♠ K J 9 8 7
♡ J 10 4 2
◇ 10 4 3
♣ 6

South
♠ 3
♡ 9 5
◇ A Q J 9 2
♣ K Q 9 8 7

2.   West now has the same number of trumps as you and you dare not play a third round of trumps for fear of another spade play.

What you must do is assume that West has the ♡ K (otherwise the hand cannot be made) and take the heart finesse immediately. When this works, cash the ♡ A, and begin to run diamonds through West. With the ♣ 10 still in dummy, all West can take is the ♣ A.

KEY LESSON POINTERS

1. WHEN YOU NEED A FINESSE TO WORK TO LAND YOUR CONTRACT, ASSUME IT WORKS AND TAKE IT. PARTNER WILL UNDERSTAND IF IT LOSES. HE WILL NEVER UNDERSTAND IF YOU FAIL TO TAKE A WINNING FINESSE. NEVER.

2. WHEN AN OPPONENT HAS THE SAME NUMBER OF TRUMPS AS YOU, ONE A HIGH TRUMP AND THE OTHER A LOW ONE, IT MAY BE IMPOSSIBLE TO KNOCK OUT THE HIGH TRUMP. IN THAT CASE YOU MUST ARRANGE TO PLAY WINNING CARDS THROUGH THIS DEFENDER WHILE LEAVING AT LEAST ONE MIDDLING TRUMP SITTING BEHIND HIM.

3. PLAYING A SECOND LOW TRUMP FROM DUMMY RATHER THAN THE ♣ 10 RE-QUIRES A LITTLE FORESIGHT. HOWEVER, A BORN PESSIMIST IS LIKELY TO GET THIS RIGHT AS HE ALWAYS ANTICIPATES THE WORST BREAKS POSSIBLE AND TAKES OUT A LITTLE INSURANCE.

4. FINALLY, BEFORE YOU PLAY WINNING CARDS THROUGH A DEFENDER THAT HAS THE TRUMPS, YOU MUST ANTICIPATE THAT HE MAY DISCARD RATHER THAN TRUMP. THAT IS WHY YOU CASHED YOUR HEARTS EARLY — YOU DIDN'T WANT WEST TO DISCARD HEARTS ON DIAMONDS. DOES YOUR PARTNER REALIZE HOW WELL YOU PLAY?

(31) JUMP REBID

East-West vulnerable
Dealer South

North
♠ K Q
♡ 4
◇ 8 7 6 3 2
♣ J 8 5 3 2

South
♠ J 10 9
♡ A Q J 7 6 5 2
◇ A
♣ Q 9

South	West	North	East
1 ♡	Pass	1 NT	Pass
3 ♡	All Pass		

Opening Lead: ◇ 5 (Third highest from four or
low from odd)

East plays the ◇ 10 which you cleverly gobble up. What do you cleverly play at trick two?

JUMP REBID (SOLUTION)

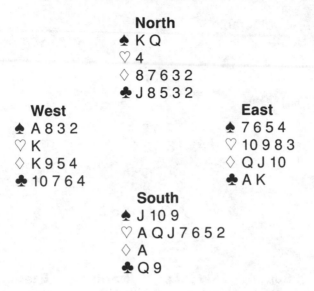

North
- ♠ K Q
- ♡ 4
- ◇ 8 7 6 3 2
- ♣ J 8 5 3 2

West
- ♠ A 8 3 2
- ♡ K
- ◇ K 9 5 4
- ♣ 10 7 6 4

East
- ♠ 7 6 5 4
- ♡ 10 9 8 3
- ◇ Q J 10
- ♣ A K

South
- ♠ J 10 9
- ♡ A Q J 7 6 5 2
- ◇ A
- ♣ Q 9

The ♡ A. You have three black suit losers and must hold your trump losses to one trick. If either opponent has four hearts headed by the king there is nothing you can do. If hearts are 3-2 you have little to worry about. The only critical holding is when West has a singleton king of hearts. In that one case you save a trick (and your contract) by leading the ♡ A.

Yes, even this safety play can go wrong. If East has ♡ Kx along with four clubs he can arrange to give West an overruff on the third round of clubs. This is a parlay to which you are going to have to pay off.

KEY LESSON POINTERS

1. KEEP THE BALL IN SIGHT. GO FOR THE PLAY THAT IS MOST LIKELY TO INSURE YOUR CONTRACT. WHEN YOU ARE PLAYING IN A TOURNAMENT YOU CAN START WORRYING ABOUT OVERTRICKS.
2. THE BEST PLAY FOR ONE LOSER WITH AQJxxxx FACING A SINGLETON IS TO PLUNK DOWN THE ACE. IF YOU CANNOT AFFORD TO LOSE A TRICK, TAKE THE FINESSE AND HOPE YOUR RIGHT HAND OPPONENT HAS Kx. (A LITTLE LESS THAN 14% — GOOD LUCK.)

(32) TECHNIQUE (1)

East-West vulnerable
Dealer South

North
♠ 10 6
♡ 10 4 3
♢ K 10
♣ A J 10 5 4 3

South
♠ K 7 3
♡ A K 6
♢ A Q J
♣ 9 8 6 2

South	West	North	East
1 NT	Pass	3 NT	All Pass

Opening Lead: ♡ Q

1.   East plays the ♡ 5. Which heart do you play? Why?
    You should win the trick with the ♡ K. Now, if East gets
the lead, he cannot be sure whether or not you have another heart stopper. If you win the trick with the ♡ A, East
knows that you remain with the ♡ K. If he gets on lead in
clubs he may switch to a dreaded spade honor.
2.   At trick two you lead a low club and West plays the ♣ Q.
Plan the play.

TECHNIQUE (SOLUTION)

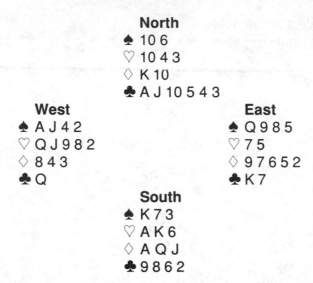

North
♠ 10 6
♡ 10 4 3
♢ K 10
♣ A J 10 5 4 3

West
♠ A J 4 2
♡ Q J 9 8 2
♢ 8 4 3
♣ Q

East
♠ Q 9 8 5
♡ 7 5
♢ 9 7 6 5 2
♣ K 7

South
♠ K 7 3
♡ A K 6
♢ A Q J
♣ 9 8 6 2

2.   Duck the ♣ Q. You would much rather have West on lead than East. East is the danger hand and could give you trouble with a switch to the jack or queen of spades.

If you play the ♣ A and another club, East will win and West might discard a heart. Now it will be easier for East to find the killing shift.

Of course, when you duck the ♣ Q, East can overtake and switch to a high spade, but some players would not overtake their partner's trick at gun point. Besides, if you never give your opponents a chance to err, they never will.

KEY LESSON POINTERS

1. IF YOU HOLD THE ACE AND KING OF A SUIT AT NO TRUMP, IT IS FAR MORE DECEPTIVE TO WIN THE TRICK WITH THE KING, PARTICULARLY IF YOU FEAR A SHIFT TO ANOTHER SUIT. YOUR RIGHT HAND OPPONENT MAY THINK THAT HIS PARTNER HAS LED FROM AN AQJ COMBINATION.
2. DON'T MAKE LIFE TOO EASY FOR YOUR OPPONENTS. GIVE THEM A CHANCE TO GO WRONG. YOU WILL BE SURPRISED HOW OFTEN THEY DO.
3. IT IS BETTER TO MAKE YOUR CRITICAL PLAYS EARLY IN THE HAND BEFORE THE OPPONENTS CAN MAKE TELLING DISCARDS. IN THIS CASE, PLAYING TWO ROUNDS OF CLUBS WOULD ALLOW WEST TO DISCARD A HEART WHICH IN TURN WOULD MAKE IT EASIER FOR EAST TO SHIFT TO A SPADE.

(33) FLANNERY

East-West vulnerable
Dealer North

North
♠ 9 7 4 2
♡ A K Q J 5
◇ K 7 2
♣ K

South
♠ Q J 10 8 5
♡ 7 6 3
◇ Q 10 9 6 3
♣ —

North	East	South	West
2 ◇*	Pass	4 ♠	All Pass

*Five hearts and four spades 11-15 H.C.P.

Opening Lead: ♣ Q

You ruff the opening lead and play the ♠ Q. West wins the king and shifts to a heart. You win in dummy and play a second spade to East's ace, West discarding a club.

East exits with a spade and West discards another club. When you test the hearts you find that East has two and West three. How do you play the diamonds?

FLANNERY (SOLUTION)

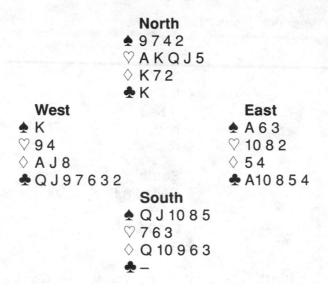

North
♠ 9 7 4 2
♡ A K Q J 5
◇ K 7 2
♣ K

West
♠ K
♡ 9 4
◇ A J 8
♣ Q J 9 7 6 3 2

East
♠ A 6 3
♡ 10 8 2
◇ 5 4
♣ A10 8 5 4

South
♠ Q J 10 8 5
♡ 7 6 3
◇ Q 10 9 6 3
♣ —

Your system has worked well here. You are on a guess for 4 ♡ and the opponents are down only one in 5 ♣.

West has turned up with one spade and three hearts. With eight clubs he might have ventured into the bidding. If West has seven clubs he has three diamonds and if he has six clubs he has four diamonds. On a percentage basis you should play West for the ◇ J.

On a psychological basis you should also play West for the ◇ J. On lead with the ♠ K, a diamond shift looks natural, yet West shifted to a heart. Why?

Either he was looking at the ◇ A Jx and was afraid to shift or, perhaps, he was playing you for 5-4-4-0 distribution and was hoping to give his partner an eventual heart ruff.

The clues all point to West having the ◇ J.

KEY LESSON POINTERS

1. WHEN A DEFENDER DOESN'T MAKE THE OBVIOUS SHIFT, HE IS PROBABLY LOOKING AT A HOLDING HE DOESN'T RELISH LEADING FROM.
2. WHEN PUSH COMES TO SHOVE, ASSUME THE PLAYER WHO HAS THE LENGTH IN THE CRITICAL SUIT (HERE, DIAMONDS) HAS THE IMPORTANT MISSING CARD.

(34) PUSHY, PUSHY (1) (2)

North-South vulnerable
Dealer East

North
♠ Q J 10 9 6
♡ J 10 8 7
◇ 9 3
♣ Q J

South
♠ A 4 3 2
♡ A 6 4
◇ A K J 2
♣ 6 3

East	South	West	North
Pass	1 NT	Pass	2 ♣
Pass	2 ♣	Pass	3 ♠
Pass	4 ♠	All Pass	

Opening Lead: ♣ 10

East takes the first two tricks with the ♣ K and ♣ A and shifts to the ◇ 7.
1.   Which diamond do you play, and what is your plan?
     You win the ◇ A, cash the ◇ K and ruff a low diamond trying to get to dummy to take the spade finesse.
     When you do this, East follows with the ◇ 6 and ◇ 5 and West plays high-low, eventually playing the 10 when you ruff the third diamond.
2.   In dummy, you lead the ♠ Q which holds, and continue with the ♠ J. East covers and West follows. Now what?
     You lead the ◇ J; West covers; you ruff, and East discards a club. Next, you run the ♡ J; East plays low and West wins the ♡ K and exits with a low heart.
3.   Which heart do you play from dummy?

PUSHY PUSHY (SOLUTION)

North
♠ Q J 10 9 6
♡ J 10 8 7
♢ 9 3
♣ Q J

West
♠ 8 7
♡ K Q 5
♢ Q 10 8 4
♣ 10 9 8 7

East
♠ K 5
♡ 9 3 2
♢ 7 6 5
♣ A K 5 4 2

South
♠ A 4 3 2
♡ A 6 4
♢ A K J 2
♣ 6 3

3.   The ♡ 10. East has already turned up with 7 high card points in clubs along with the ♠ K. With the ♡ Q as well, East would have opened the bidding.

KEY LESSON POINTERS

1. IF POSSIBLE, STRIP THE HAND BEFORE YOU ATTACK THE CRITICAL SUIT. HAD YOU NEGLECTED TO RUFF YOUR FOURTH DIAMOND BEFORE RUNNING THE ♡ J, WEST COULD HAVE EXITED SAFELY WITH THE ♢ Q AFTER WINNING A HEART TRICK.
2. WATCH THE HIGH CARDS AS THEY FALL FROM THE OPPONENTS' HANDS. AS-SUME THAT A PLAYER WILL OPEN THE BIDDING WITH 12 HIGH CARD POINTS. IF A PASSED HAND TURNS UP WITH 10 HIGH CARD POINTS, PLAY HIS PART-NER FOR ANY OTHER MISSING ACE, KING, OR QUEEN.
3. THE TEN. EAST HAS ALREADY TURNED UP WITH 10 HIGH CARD POINTS IN THE BLACK SUITS. IF EAST HAD A HEART HONOR HE WOULD HAVE OPENED THE BIDDING. YES, EAST COULD HAVE DEFEATED THE CONTRACT BY SHIFTING TO A HEART AT TRICK THREE RATHER THAN A DIAMOND. WHY NOT TELL EAST THAT AND MAKE A FRIEND FOR LIFE?

(35) THIS IS BIDDING?

North-South vulnerable
Dealer West

North
♠ J 6 3
♡ A K J 5
◇ A K 7 6 5
♣ A

South
♠ A 8 4
♡ 8 6
◇ J 4 3 2
♣ K Q 10 7

West	North	East	South
2 ♠*	Dbl.	Pass	3 NT
Pass	6 NT	All Pass	

*Weak

Opening Lead: ♠ K

East plays the ♠ 2. What is your plan?

THIS IS BIDDING? (SOLUTION)

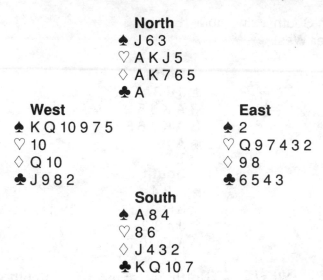

North
♠ J 6 3
♡ A K J 5
◇ A K 7 6 5
♣ A

West
♠ K Q 10 9 7 5
♡ 10
◇ Q 10
♣ J 9 8 2

East
♠ 2
♡ Q 9 7 4 3 2
◇ 9 8
♣ 6 5 4 3

South
♠ A 8 4
♡ 8 6
◇ J 4 3 2
♣ K Q 10 7

Forget the bidding on this hand. It's a play problem. You must assume you are going to take five diamond tricks, and if you do, you have twelve tricks — two spades, two hearts, five diamonds and three clubs. But there is a catch.

The catch is that you must lead a spade at trick two and develop your twelfth trick in spades before you unblock the clubs.

If you lead a spade at once, the best the defense can do is win the trick and play a heart.   You win, cash the ♣ A and the top diamonds, enter your hand with the ◇ J, cash your clubs etc. Twelve tricks.

Now look what happens if you cross to the ♣ A prematurely. When you eventually reenter your hand with the ◇ J, your last hand entry, you must cash your clubs. Now when you lead up to the ♠ J, West wins and cashes the ♣ J. For shame.

KEY LESSON POINTERS

1. WHEN DEALING WITH A BLOCKED SUIT AND A PRECARIOUS ENTRY SITUATION, YOU MUST NOT SQUANDER YOUR ENTRY PREMATURELY.
2. IF YOU FAILED TO LEAD A SPADE AT TRICK TWO, YOU DID NOT LOOK INTO THE HAND DEEPLY ENOUGH.
3. IN GENERAL, DEVELOP TRICKS EARLY WHILE RETAINING CONTROL OF THE OTHER SUITS AND MAINTAINING A FLUID ENTRY ARRANGEMENT.
4. WHEN YOU NEED A SUIT TO COME IN FOR THE MAXIMUM NUMBER OF TRICKS IN ORDER TO MAKE YOUR CONTRACT, ASSUME IT WILL, AND PLAY ACCORDINGLY.

(36) A BREATHER

Neither side vulnerable
Dealer East

North
♠ A K Q 6 4
♡ K 9 8 4
◇ J
♣ K J 5

South
♠ 9
♡ A J 10 7 5 3
◇ K Q 10 8
♣ 10 3

East	South	West	North
Pass	1 ♡	3 ♣*	4 NT
Pass	5 ◇	Pass	5 ♡
All Pass			

*Weak

Opening Lead: ♣ A   East plays the ♣ 4

What is your plan — which hand do you play for the ♡ Q, etc?

A BREATHER (SOLUTION)

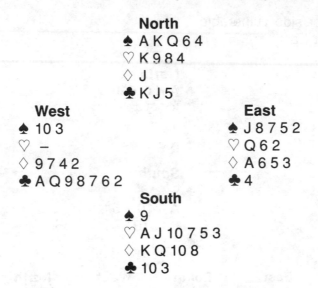

North
♠ A K Q 6 4
♡ K 9 8 4
◇ J
♣ K J 5

West
♠ 10 3
♡ –
◇ 9 7 4 2
♣ A Q 9 8 7 6 2

East
♠ J 8 7 5 2
♡ Q 6 2
◇ A 6 5 3
♣ 4

South
♠ 9
♡ A J 10 7 5 3
◇ K Q 10 8
♣ 10 3

The ♡ Q is the least of your problems; the danger of a club ruff is what should be worrying you. You must play the ♣ 10 at trick one so that West, if he holds seven clubs, will not know for sure whether or not his partner started with a singleton club.

If you can survive trick two, you should play East for the ♡ Q. As West is known to have length in clubs, he figures to be the one that is shorter in hearts.

KEY LESSON POINTERS

1. A PRIMARY (AND MANDATORY) WINNING TECHNIQUE FOR DECLARER IS TO RETAIN LOW SPOT CARDS TO CONFUSE THE ENEMY SIGNALING. BY RETAINING CARDS LOWER THAN THE ONE THAT HAS BEEN LED, OR LOWER THAN THE ONE THAT THIRD HAND HAS PLAYED, YOU BOTH CONFUSE THE COUNT AND THE ATTITUDE SIGNALING OF THE OPPONENTS.
2. WHEN ONE PLAYER IS KNOWN TO BE LONG IN ONE SUIT, THAT PLAYER SHOULD BE ASSUMED TO BE SHORTER THAN HIS PARTNER IN ANY OTHER PARTICULAR SUIT. LENGTH ATTRACTS SHORTNESS AND SHORTNESS ATTRACTS LENGTH.

(37) THINKING AHEAD (1)

East-West vulnerable
Dealer South

North
♠ J 2
♡ A K 10 6 4
◇ Q 4
♣ A Q J 4

South
♠ A Q 10 9 4 3
♡ 5 3 2
◇ J 10
♣ 10 2

South	West	North	East
2 ♠*	Pass	4 ♠	All Pass
*Weak			

Opening Lead: ◇ 6

East wins the ◇ A and returns the ◇ 3 to West's king. At trick three West shifts to the ♡ 7.
1.   Which heart do you play from dummy?
You win with the ace or king, as East plays the ♡ 9.
2.   What is your plan from here?

THINKING AHEAD (SOLUTION)

North
♠ J 2
♡ A K 10 6 4
◇ Q 4
♣ A Q J 4

West
♠ K 8 7
♡ Q 8 7
◇ K 9 7 6
♣ K 6 3

East
♠ 6 5
♡ J 9
◇ A 8 5 3 2
♣ 9 8 7 5

South
♠ A Q 10 9 4 3
♡ 5 3 2
◇ J 10
♣ 10 2

2.   Lead the ♠ J from dummy. If East plays low, overtake with the ♠ Q, a key play. If the ♠ Q holds, you are now in your hand to take the club finesse, a finesse that is virtually a cinch to work given that West did not shift to a club at trick three.

If the club finesse loses, you still have the repeat spade finesse in reserve.

The trap is running the ♠ J without covering. If the ♠ J holds, and you lead a second spade to the queen, a wily West might win this trick and return a heart. Now you are locked in dummy and cannot take the club finesse, let alone draw the last trump.

True, you could win the second round of spades with the ace and take the club finesse, but wouldn't you look silly if East had both black kings? No sense trusting your opponents if you don't have to.

KEY LESSON POINTERS

1. WHEN A DEFENDER DOES NOT MAKE THE OBVIOUS SHIFT THROUGH AN ACE-QUEEN COMBINATION IN DUMMY, ASSUME THAT DEFENDER EITHER HAS THE KING OR DID NOT GET A GOOD NIGHT'S SLEEP.

2. WHEN DUMMY HAS TWO TRUMPS, YOU MUST BE PREPARED FOR AN EXPERT DEFENDER SITTING BEHIND YOU TO WIN THE SECOND ROUND OF TRUMPS RATHER THAN THE FIRST. BY WINNING THE SECOND ROUND, HE MAY MAKE IT DIFFICULT FOR YOU TO RETURN TO YOUR HAND TO DRAW THE REMAINING TRUMP(S).

3. IN ORDER TO CREATE A CERTAIN ENTRY TO YOUR OWN HAND IN THE TRUMP SUIT, IT MAY BE NECESSARY TO OVERTAKE AN HONOR FROM DUMMY —PROVIDING YOU HAVE THE SPOTS TO DO SO. HERE YOU DO.

(38) 100 HONORS

East-West vulnerable
Dealer South

North
♠ 9 8 2
♡ 7 4 3
◇ A K 6 5
♣ 7 4 3

South
♠ A K J 10 5
♡ A K 8 5
◇ Q J
♣ J 8

South	West	North	East
1 ♠	Pass	1 NT	Pass
3 ♡	Pass	3 ♠	Pass
3 NT	Pass	4 ♠	All Pass

Opening Lead: ♣ A (A from AK)

East signals with the ♣ 9, and West continues with the king and a low club to East's queen. Plan your play from here.

100 HONORS (SOLUTION)

North
♠ 9 8 2
♡ 7 4 3
◇ A K 6 5
♣ 7 4 3

<table>
<tr><td>West</td><td>East</td></tr>
<tr><td>♠ Q 7 3</td><td>♠ 6 4</td></tr>
<tr><td>♡ J 9 2</td><td>♡ Q 10 6</td></tr>
<tr><td>◇ 9 3 2</td><td>◇ 10 8 7 4</td></tr>
<tr><td>♣ A K 10 5</td><td>♣ Q 9 6 2</td></tr>
</table>

South
♠ A K J 10 5
♡ A K 8 5
◇ Q J
♣ J 8

You should ruff the club with the ♠ 10 and exit with the ♠ J. Assuming spades to be 3-2, somebody will win the ♠ Q and, regardless of the return, you have ten tricks. You will be able to discard two losing hearts on your winning diamonds after unblocking the suit. Dummy's ♠ 9 is the entry to the diamonds, of course.

Taking the spade finesse is definitely an inferior play.

KEY LESSON POINTERS

1. BLOCKED SUITS (DIAMONDS) CREATE CERTAIN ENTRY PROBLEMS.
2. AT TIMES, CONCEDING A TRICK THAT MAY NOT OTHERWISE HAVE TO BE LOST IN ORDER TO CREATE A CERTAIN ENTRY IS THE BEST WAY TO HANDLE THE BLOCKAGE.
3. SOUTH'S BIDDING HAS DESCRIBED A 5-4-2-2 DISTRIBUTION. NORTH MAY HAVE HAD A DOUBLETON SPADE AND PREFERRED 3NT AFTER ALL.
4. IF, AFTER RUFFING THE CLUB WITH A SPADE HONOR AT TRICK THREE, YOU LEAD A HIGH SPADE AND THEN YOUR REMAINING MIDDLE SPADE HONOR AT TRICKS FOUR AND FIVE, A CLEVER DEFENDER WITH ♠ Qxx COULD WIN THE QUEEN AND RETURN A SPADE WHILE THE DIAMONDS ARE BLOCKED.
   IF YOU UNBLOCK THE DIAMONDS BEFORE CONCEDING A SPADE, A 5-2 DIAMOND DIVISION COULD LEAD TO TROUBLE.

(39) PRECISION NOTRUMP (1) (2)

East-West vulnerable
Dealer South

North
♠ Q 10 9 8 7
♡ Q 10 5 4
♢ 2
♣ A J 10

South
♠ A K 3 2
♡ 9 3
♢ K Q J 9
♣ Q 9 8

South	West	North	East
1 NT*	Pass	2 ♣	2 ♡
2 ♠	Pass	3 ♠	Pass
4 ♠	All Pass		
*13-15			

Opening Lead: ♡ 2

East wins the first trick with the ♡ J and cashes the ♡ K, West discarding the ♣ 2. East continues with a low heart which you ruff high, West discarding the ♣ 6.
1.   What is your next play?
     You lead a low spade to the seven which holds, East following.
2.   What is your next play?
     You lead a diamond from dummy to the king and West's ace.
3.   West shifts to a club. How do you proceed?

PRECISION NOTRUMP (SOLUTION)

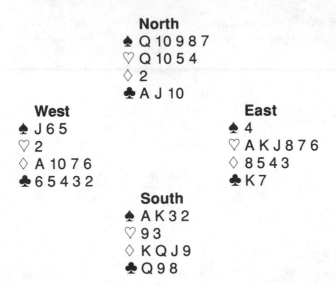

North
♠ Q 10 9 8 7
♡ Q 10 5 4
◇ 2
♣ A J 10

West
♠ J 6 5
♡ 2
◇ A 10 7 6
♣ 6 5 4 3 2

East
♠ 4
♡ A K J 8 7 6
◇ 8 5 4 3
♣ K 7

South
♠ A K 3 2
♡ 9 3
◇ K Q J 9
♣ Q 9 8

3.   Win the ♣ A, ruff dummy's last heart high, cash your two winning diamonds, discarding clubs from the dummy, and finesse in trumps one last time.

KEY LESSON POINTERS

1. A PLAYER WHO INTERVENES AT UNFAVORABLE VULNERABILITY BETWEEN TWO BIDDERS AT THE TWO LEVEL WITH A BROKEN SIX CARD SUIT SHOULD HAVE SOME SIDE DISTRIBUTION. HE IS A FAVORITE TO HAVE A SIDE SINGLETON.

2. SOUTH CAN ASSUME THAT WEST MUST HAVE THE ACE OF DIAMONDS IF EAST HAS THE ♣ K. IF EAST HAD BOTH OF THOSE CARDS, HE WOULD HAVE LED A LOW HEART AT TRICK TWO FOR PARTNER TO RUFF AND RETURN A CLUB. IF EAST HAD THE ◇ A AND NO ♣ K, HE PROBABLY WOULD HAVE CASHED THE ◇ A BEFORE LEADING A THIRD HEART.

3. WHEN THE DUMMY HAS MORE TRUMPS THAN YOU DO, ASSUME THE DUMMY IS THE MASTER HAND AND THINK OF GETTING RID OF DUMMY'S LOSERS RATHER THAN VICE VERSA.

4. HAD WEST DISCARDED DIAMONDS RATHER THAN CLUBS ON THE HEART PLAYS, YOUR COUNTER WOULD BE TO DRAW TRUMPS (ENDING IN YOUR HAND) AFTER WINNING THE ♣ A. NOW YOU MUST HOPE THAT YOUR ◇ 9 HAS BEEN ESTABLISHED FOR YOUR TENTH TRICK.

(40) NINE-WORKING ON TEN (1)

East-West vulnerable
Dealer South

North
♠ Q J 6 4
♡ A 9 3
◇ 10 8 2
♣ A 7 4

South
♠ 2
♡ K Q J 10 8 6 5
◇ A Q 4
♣ J 2

South	West	North	East
1 ♡	Dbl.	Rdbl.	1 ♠
3 ♡	Pass	4 ♡	All Pass

Opening Lead: ♣ K

1. Do you win this trick or do you play low? Why?
    It can't hurt to duck. West may shift to a diamond.
2. No such luck. West shifts to a trump, East follows. How
    do you continue?

NINE-WORKING ON TEN (SOLUTION)

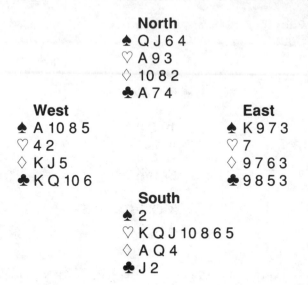

North
♠ Q J 6 4
♡ A 9 3
♢ 10 8 2
♣ A 7 4

West
♠ A 10 8 5
♡ 4 2
♢ K J 5
♣ K Q 10 6

East
♠ K 9 7 3
♡ 7
♢ 9 7 6 3
♣ 9 8 5 3

South
♠ 2
♡ K Q J 10 8 6 5
♢ A Q 4
♣ J 2

You have a near lock. Cash a second high trump, cross to the ♣ A, ruff a club, and exit a spade.

If West wins he is endplayed. If East wins and makes his best return of a diamond, duck the trick into West.

Even if West has both missing diamond honors he is endplayed upon winning this trick. Presumably West has one missing spade honor to justify his take-out double so he cannot lead that suit. A diamond lead goes into your AQ, and a club gives you a ruff and a sluff. West has no answer.

KEY LESSON POINTERS

1. HOLDING Axx IN DUMMY FACING Jx IN THE CLOSED HAND, IT IS USUALLY RIGHT TO PLAY LOW FROM DUMMY IF THE KING IS LED. IT IS OFTEN DIFFICULT FOR THE OPENING LEADER TO WORK OUT THAT THE JACK IS BARE AND HE MAY SHIFT TO ANOTHER SUIT.
2. IN GENERAL, WHEN DECLARER HAS A CHOICE OF SUITS TO ATTACK HE SHOULD CONCENTRATE ON UNEVENLY DIVIDED SUITS (SPADES) RATHER THAN EVENLY DIVIDED SUITS (DIAMONDS).
3. BY DRAWING THE OPPONENTS' TRUMPS AND STRIPPING THE MEANINGLESS SUIT (CLUBS), DECLARER CAN FORCE THE OPPONENTS TO PLAY SUITS HE WOULD RATHER NOT BROACH HIMSELF.
4. IF EAST RETURNS A SPADE UPON WINNING THE KING OF SPADES, DISCARD A DIAMOND AND THEN DISCARD THE OTHER DIAMOND ON DUMMY'S ESTABLISHED SPADE. A CLASSIC LOSER ON LOSER PLAY.

(41) PRESSURE (1)

Neither side vulnerable
Dealer East

North
♠ K 7 4
♡ A Q 8
◇ 7 4 2
♣ Q 8 4 3

South
♠ A Q 9 5
♡ J 10 3
◇ K Q 10
♣ A 7 5

East	South	West	North
1 ◇	1 NT	Pass	3 NT
All Pass			

Opening Lead: ◇ 9

You win the first trick with the ◇ 10; East signals with the ◇ 8.
1. How do you begin?
    You lead a low heart to the queen and king, West playing the ♡ 2.
2. East continues with the ace and a diamond; West discards a second heart on the third round of diamonds. Now what?

PRESSURE (SOLUTION)

North
♠ K 7 4
♡ A Q 8
◇ 7 4 2
♣ Q 8 4 3

West
♠ 10 8 6 2
♡ 7 5 2
◇ 9 3
♣ J 9 6 2

East
♠ J 3
♡ K 9 6 4
◇ A J 8 6 5
♣ K 10

South
♠ A Q 9 5
♡ J 10 3
◇ K Q 10
♣ A 7 5

1.   Play two more rounds of hearts before you test the spades. One never knows, perhaps some unsuspecting soul will discard a spade on the third round of hearts.

Look at the actual layout. West must make a discard on the third heart. Holding four clubs and four spades he may go wrong. It goes without saying that there is no point in attacking clubs because East is marked with the king.

KEY LESSON POINTERS

1. WHEN YOU HAVE REACHED A POINT IN THE PLAY OF THE HAND WHERE YOU CAN NO LONGER DEVELOP ANY EXTRA TRICKS AND ARE REDUCED TO RELYING ON A 3-3 BREAK IN A SIDE SUIT, IT IS USUALLY RIGHT TO CASH YOUR ESTABLISHED WINNERS IN THE OTHER SUITS. A FAULTY DISCARD FROM AN UNSUSPECTING OPPONENT COULD ESTABLISH AN EXTRA TRICK FOR YOU.

2. IF YOU HOLD J10x FACING AQx AND YOU WANT TO SMOKE OUT THE KING. LEAD LOW TO THE QUEEN. IF YOU RUN THE JACK INSTEAD, IT IS MUCH EASIER FOR FOURTH HAND TO DUCK.

3. IT IS BETTER TO OVERCALL ONE NOTRUMP THAN TO MAKE A TAKEOUT DOUBLE WHEN HOLDING A BALANCED HAND ALONG WITH TWO STOPPERS IN THE ENEMY SUIT. (IT IS USUALLY RIGHT WITH ONLY ONE STOPPER.) IT SIMPLIFIES THE BIDDING. PARTNER CAN STILL USE STAYMAN TO UNCOVER A POSSIBLE 4-4 MAJOR SUIT FIT.

(42) FASHIONABLE OVERCALL

Neither side vulnerable
Dealer South

North
♠ 9 7 3 2
♡ J 2
◇ A K 7 6 3 2
♣ A

South
♠ 6 5
♡ A Q 10 9 4
◇ J
♣ K Q J 10 5

South	West	North	East
1 ♡	1 ♠	2 ◇	Pass
2 ♡	Pass	4 ♡	All Pass

Opening Lead: ♠ K

West continues with the ♠ Q and a third spade to East's ♠ A which you ruff low.

What is the safest line of play to bring in the contract?

FASHIONABLE OVERCALL (SOLUTION)

North
♠ 9 7 3 2
♡ J 2
◊ A K 7 6 3 2
♣ A

West
♠ K Q J 10
♡ K 8
◊ Q 5 4
♣ 9 8 7 6

East
♠ A 8 4
♡ 7 6 5 3
◊ 10 9 8
♣ 4 3 2

South
♠ 6 5
♡ A Q 10 9 4
◊ J
♣ K Q J 10 5

East's failure to raise to 2 ♠ with Axx in support of partner's suit suggests a balanced hand with no other facecards.

If East's four card suit is hearts, taking the heart finesse will be disastrous. West will win and play a fourth spade promoting one of East's lowly trumps to the setting trick.

A better plan is to dismiss the trump finesse and try to take ten tricks by cashing winners and trumping winners and losers. What fun!

Cash the ◊ A K and the ♣ A and ruff a diamond back to the closed hand. Next, cash the ♣ K and the ♣ J. If everyone follows, ruff the ♣ Q with the ♡ J. Trump flush, the most you can lose is the ♡ K.

If West happens to ruff the third club low, indicating a possible distribution of 4-4-3-2, overtrump with the ♡ J, ruff a spade back to your hand and play your last club. West will have to trump and be forced to lead away from his guarded ♡ K to give you the last two tricks.

KEY LESSON POINTERS

1. TWO-SUITERS OFTEN RUN INTO CONTROL PROBLEMS WHEN DECLARER IS FORCED TO RUFF IN HIS OWN HAND ONCE TOO OFTEN. IF A DEFENDER WINDS UP WITH MORE TRUMPS THAN DECLARER THAT IS USUALLY BAD NEWS — VERY BAD NEWS.

2. ONE WAY TO OVERCOME THIS PROBLEM IS TO TRY TO MAKE YOUR CONTRACT BY CASHING YOUR TOP TRICKS AND RUFFING A WINNER OR WINNERS IN DUMMY. IN ORDER TO DO THIS YOU MUST HAVE MOST OF THE HIGH TRUMPS. IT IS CALLED "SCRAMBLING" AND CAN BE VERY EFFECTIVE AGAINST AN UNEVEN TRUMP DIVISION.

3. WHEN A SILENT OPPONENT TURNS UP WITH Axx IN A MAJOR SUIT HIS PARTNER HAS OVERCALLED, ASSUME HE HAS LITTLE ELSE OF VALUE PLUS A BALANCED HAND ON THE SIDE. MOST PLAYERS WILL RAISE WITH Axx AND A SIDE DOUBLETON JUST TO GET THE LEAD. AT LEAST THE BRAVE ONES WILL . . . NOT VULNERABLE.

(43) ACTIVE OPPONENTS (1) (2)

Neither side vulnerable
Dealer South

> **North**
> ♠ 7 5 3 2
> ♡ 8 4
> ◇ K Q 9 7
> ♣ Q 7 6

> **South**
> ♠ A K J
> ♡ J
> ◇ A J 10 8 5 2
> ♣ A 4 2

South	West	North	East
1 ◇	2 ◇*	3 ◇	4 ♡
5 ◇	All Pass		

*Majors

Opening Lead: ♡ K

    East overtakes and shifts to the ♠ 8 which you win. You
draw trumps, East shedding a heart on the second round.
1.   Now what?
      You cash the ♣ A and West plays the ♣ K.
2.   What is your next play?
      You cross to the ♣ Q, West following.
3.   Now what?

ACTIVE OPPONENTS (SOLUTION)

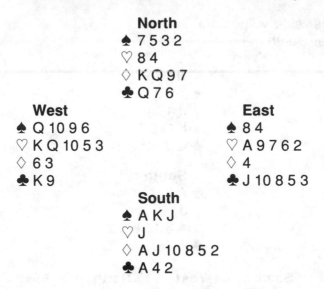

North
♠ 7 5 3 2
♡ 8 4
◇ K Q 9 7
♣ Q 7 6

West
♠ Q 10 9 6
♡ K Q 10 5 3
◇ 6 3
♣ K 9

East
♠ 8 4
♡ A 9 7 6 2
◇ 4
♣ J 10 8 5 3

South
♠ A K J
♡ J
◇ A J 10 8 5 2
♣ A 4 2

1.   Ruff a heart, cash a second winning spade and exit with a club. East will have to win and give you a ruff and a sluff, allowing you to trump your losing spade.

KEY LESSON POINTERS

1. WHEN A PLAYER INDICATES A TWO-SUITER WITH A CONVENTIONAL BID, HIS DIS-TRIBUTION WILL USUALLY BE AT LEAST 5-5. AN OCCASIONAL 5-4 EXCEPTION IS MADE WITH THE MAJORS, NON-VULNERABLE.
2. IN ORDER FOR YOU TO MAKE THIS HAND, WEST MUST HAVE THE ♣ K, SO PLAY HIM FOR IT.
3. ONCE WEST TURNS UP WITH A SECOND CLUB HE IS KNOWN TO HAVE STARTED WITH EITHER 5-4-2-2 or 4-5-2-2. IN EITHER CASE IT IS SAFE TO CASH A SECOND SPADE BEFORE EXITING A CLUB.
4. EQUAL LENGTH SUITS, SUCH AS CLUBS, LEND THEMSELVES TO THROW-IN POSSI-BILITIES. BEFORE ATTACKING AN EQUAL LENGTH SUIT, TRY TO EITHER STRIP, OR PARTIALLY STRIP, THE HAND.

(44) NINE SURE TRICKS

East-West vulnerable
Dealer South

North
♠ 3 2
♡ K Q 10 8
◇ A 10 7 5
♣ 8 5 4

South
♠ A K Q J 10 9 8
♡ 2
◇ Q 8
♣ A J 6

South	West	North	East
1 ♠	Pass	1 NT	Pass
4 ♠	All Pass		Pass

Opening Lead: ◇ 2

What is your plan?

NINE SURE TRICKS (SOLUTION)

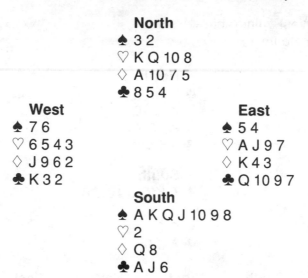

North
♠ 3 2
♡ K Q 10 8
◇ A 10 7 5
♣ 8 5 4

West
♠ 7 6
♡ 6 5 4 3
◇ J 9 6 2
♣ K 3 2

East
♠ 5 4
♡ A J 9 7
◇ K 4 3
♣ Q 10 9 7

South
♠ A K Q J 10 9 8
♡ 2
◇ Q 8
♣ A J 6

This is basically a very simple hand. You should duck the opening lead in dummy. If West has led from the ◇ K you are playing for overtricks as your contract is assured. If East produces the ◇ K, you must unblock the ◇ Q. You almost certainly will have to finesse the ◇ 10 in order to get rid of one of your losers.

If you do not unblock the ◇ Q, and East makes his normal shift to a middle club, you will lose four tricks without being able to do too much about it.

KEY LESSON POINTERS

1. WHEN YOU HOLD A DOUBLETON HONOR FACING HONOR-TEN WITH LENGTH IN DUMMY AND NO CERTAIN OUTSIDE ENTRY, IT IS ALMOST ALWAYS RIGHT TO UNBLOCK THE HONOR FROM THE DOUBLETON SIDE EARLY.

HERE IS ONE COMMON POSITION:

North
♠ Q 10 3

West
♠ J 9 4 2

East
♠ A 8 6 5

South
♠ K 7

WEST LEADS THE ♠ 2, DUMMY PLAYS LOW AND EAST PLAYS THE ♠ A. IF THE DUMMY HAS NO CERTAIN ENTRY, SOUTH MUST UNBLOCK THE KING AND LATER FINESSE THE TEN TO TAKE TWO TRICKS. THE FINESSE IS PRACTICALLY A CERTAINTY — IF EAST HAD AJx(x), EAST WOULD HAVE PLAYED THE JACK THE FIRST TIME THE SUIT WAS LED.

HERE IS ANOTHER COMMON POSITION:

North
♠ A 10 4

West
♠ Q 7 6 5 2

East
♠ K 8 3

South
♠ J 9

WEST LEADS LOW AND EAST WINS THE KING. SOUTH SHOULD, AS A MATTER OF COURSE, UNBLOCK THE JACK TO BE A BLE TO FINESSE THE TEN LATER — A FINESSE THAT IS ALMOST CERTAIN TO WORK. SOUTH WOULD MAKE THE SAME UNBLOCK WITH Q9 IF DUMMY HAD NO SIDE ENTRY. AFTER THE UNBLOCK, SOUTH CAN FINESSE THE TEN IF HE WISHES.

(45) TEN CARD FIT (2)

East-West vulnerable
Dealer South

North
♠ Q 7 6 3 2
♡ K 9 8 7
◇ 10 5 4
♣ 10

South
♠ 8 5
♡ A Q J 6 3 2
◇ K 3
♣ A Q 6

South	West	North	East
1 ♡	1 ♠	3 ♡*	Pass
4 ♡	All Pass		

*Preemptive Jump Raise in competition.

Opening Lead: ♡ 10

1.   How do you visualize the spade suit?
2.   How do you begin?

You win in dummy and lead a diamond to the king and ace.

3.   West continues with the ◇ Q and a third diamond which you ruff. Now what?

TEN CARD FIT (SOLUTION)

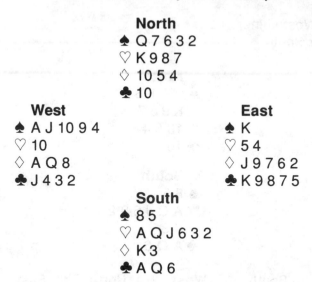

North
♠ Q 7 6 3 2
♡ K 9 8 7
◇ 10 5 4
♣ 10

West
♠ A J 10 9 4
♡ 10
◇ A Q 8
♣ J 4 3 2

East
♠ K
♡ 5 4
◇ J 9 7 6 2
♣ K 9 8 7 5

South
♠ 8 5
♡ A Q J 6 3 2
◇ K 3
♣ A Q 6

1.   East is marked with a singleton king or ace. West should have a five card suit for his vulnerable overcall, and would certainly have led a high spade holding both the ace and king. Wouldn't you?
2.   Your only chance is to try to strip the hand before leading a spade. Cross to dummy with a trump, lead a club to the queen, cash the ♣ A, ruff a club, and exit a spade.

   East, perforce, will have to win the trick and give you a ruff and a sluff, allowing you to ruff in dummy while discarding your remaining spade from your hand.

KEY LESSON POINTERS

1.   IF YOU ARE TRYING TO PLACE AN ACE-KING COMBINATION IN A SIDE SUIT THAT WAS NOT LED, ASSUME THAT HONORS ARE EITHER DIVIDED OR TO YOUR RIGHT.
2.   WHEN THE SUIT HAS BEEN BID TO YOUR LEFT, ASSUME THE HONORS ARE DIVIDED. IN THIS CASE, NOT ONLY DO YOU KNOW THE SPADE HONORS ARE DIVIDED, BUT YOU ALSO KNOW THAT EAST HAS A SINGLETON HONOR.
3.   IN ORDER TO TAKE ADVANTAGE OF AN ADVERSELY BLOCKED SUIT, STRIP THE HAND BEFORE PLAYING THE SUIT.
4.   AN EXPERT PLAYER TRIES TO PLAY THE HAND MENTALLY BEFORE ACTUALLY TOUCHING A CARD. FOR EXAMPLE, IF YOU HAD DRAWN A SECOND ROUND OF TRUMPS PREMATURELY, YOU WOULD HAVE BEEN SHORT AN ENTRY TO DUMMY FOR THE STRIPPING PROCESS. YOU ALMOST HAVE TO ENVISION THAT THE DEFENDERS WILL PLAY THREE ROUNDS OF DIAMONDS.
5.   HAD EAST DOUBLED 3 ♡, IT WOULD HAVE BEEN A TAKEOUT FOR THE UNBID SUITS — A RESPONSIVE DOUBLE. EAST WAS A LITTLE WEAK FOR THAT ACTION. AFTER PARTNER HAS MADE A SIMPLE OVERCALL, AND THE OPPONENTS HAVE SUPPORTED EACH OTHER AT THE TWO OR THREE LEVEL, A DOUBLE BY THE ADVANCER (PARTNER OF THE OVERCALLER) IS FOR TAKEOUT.

(46) THE SPADES HAVE IT (1)

Neither side vulnerable
Dealer South

North
♠ 9 6 4 2
♡ A 10 4
♢ A 5 3
♣ 10 5 4

South
♠ K Q J 10 8 3
♡ Q 7
♢ K 6 4
♣ Q 6

South	West	North	East
1 ♠	Dbl.	2 ♠	3 ♡
3 ♠	All Pass		

Opening Lead: ♢ Q

1. Where do you win this trick, and what do you play to trick two?   You win in dummy and lead a low heart.
2. East wins the ♡ K and plays back a diamond. How do you continue?

THE SPADES HAVE IT (SOLUTION)

North
♠ 9 6 4 2
♡ A 10 4
♢ A 5 3
♣ 10 5 4

West
♠ A 5
♡ J 8 3 2
♢ Q J 10
♣ A J 9 3

East
♠ 7
♡ K 9 6 5
♢ 9 8 7 2
♣ K 8 7 2

South
♠ K Q 10 8 3
♡ Q 7
♢ K 6 4
♣ Q 6

2.   If you didn't unblock the ♡ Q under the king, it won't really matter how you continue! You are destined to lose five tricks, two clubs, a diamond, a heart and a spade.

The reason you attacked hearts in the first place was to try to set up an additional heart winner before the defenders could establish their diamond winner.

Because the heart suit is blocked and there is no quick dummy entry to the ♡ A, you must unblock the ♡ Q and finesse the ♡ 10 upon winning the second diamond. It's all in the planning.

KEY LESSON POINTERS

1. COUNT YOUR LOSERS BEFORE YOU BEGIN. THEN COUNT YOUR WINNERS. THEN , AS SHEINWOLD SAYS, IF THE TOTAL DOESN'T COME TO 13, COUNT YOUR CARDS.
2. SOME LOSERS ARE FAST, SUCH AS IN CLUBS; SOME ARE SLOW, SUCH AS IN DIAMONDS.
3. WHEN YOU HAVE A SLOW LOSER YOU SHOULD TRY TO SET UP A WINNER IN ANOTHER SUIT BEFORE THE DEFENDERS CAN TURN YOUR SLOW LOSER INTO A FAST ONE. BASICALLY A RACE.
4. IF THE SUIT YOU ARE ESTABLISHING IS BLOCKED THEN YOU MUST CONSIDER UNBLOCKING THE HIGH HONOR FROM THE SHORT SIDE TO ALLOW FOR THE POSSIBILITY OF A LATER FINESSE.
5 ALTHOUGH IT LOOKS AS IF YOU NEED THE DUMMY ENTRY IN DIAMONDS, IT IS IMPORTANT TO WIN THE OPENING LEAD IN DUMMY. IF YOU WIN IN YOUR HAND, IT IS INCONVENIENT TO LEAD HEARTS. EVEN IF YOU LEAD A LOW HEART TO THE TEN AND IT DRIVES OUT THE KING, AN IMMEDIATE DIAMOND RETURN WILL LEAVE YOU IN AN UNTENABLE POSITION.

(47) CONSERVATIVE BID

North-South vulnerable
Dealer East

North
♠ A K Q J
♡ A K Q 9
◇ –
♣ A Q J 6 4

South
♠ 10 3 2
♡ 10 6 5 4
◇ 10 3 2
♣ 10 9 2

East	South	West	North
2 ◇*	Pass	3 ◇	4 ◇
Pass	4 ♡	Pass	7 ♡!
All Pass			
* Weak			

Opening Lead: ◇ 4

With which card do you ruff in dummy, and what is your plan?

CONSERVATIVE BID   (SOLUTION)

North
♠ A K Q J
♡ A K Q 9
♢ —
♣ A Q J 6 4

<table>
<tr><td>

West
♠ 7 5 4
♡ J 8 2
♢ K 7 5 4
♣ K 8 3

</td><td>

East
♠ 9 8 6
♡ 7 3
♢ A Q J 9 8 6
♣ 7 5

</td></tr>
</table>

South
♠ 10 3 2
♡ 10 6 5 4
♢ 10 3 2
♣ 10 9 2

Help! What a mess, but don't give up. Your best bet is to ruff the opening lead with the ♡ 9 and play off three rounds of trumps.

Assuming trumps have broken, play four rounds of spades and trump the fourth spade with your last heart. Now run the ♣ 10. If you have led a clean life, West will have the ♣ K doubleton or tripleton and you will chalk up a vulnerable grand slam.

KEY LESSON POINTERS

1. THERE IS NO SUCH THING AS A HOPELESS CONTRACT. SOME ARE A BIT MORE TOUCHY THAN OTHERS, THAT'S ALL.

2. DON'T WORRY ABOUT GOING DOWN FIVE OR SIX TRICKS IN A SLAM IF YOU ARE NOT DOUBLED — AS LONG AS YOUR LINE OF PLAY HAS SOME CHANCE OF SUCCESS.

3. KEEP IN MIND THAT ONE WAY OF GETTING BACK TO ONE'S HAND TO TRY A FINESSE IS TO RUFF A WINNER. IT IS A BLIND SPOT TO RUFF THE OPENING LEAD WITH AN HONOR THINKING THAT YOU NEED TO FIND THE ♡ J DOUBLETON IN ORDER TO GET BACK TO YOUR HAND WITH THE ♡ 10 TO TRY THE CLUB FINESSE.

(48) WHATTA HAND! (1)

Neither side vulnerable
Dealer West

North
♠ A J 10 4
♡ A 10 2
◇ 7 2
♣ A K Q 9

South
♠ K Q 9 7 6 5
♡ 8 7 6 5 4 3
◇ A
♣ —

West	North	East	South
Pass	1 ♣	Pass	1 ♠
Pass	4 ♠	Pass	6 ♠
All Pass			

Opening Lead: ◇ K (East plays the ◇ J)

You win and lead a trump to dummy, all following.
1. What is your plan?
    You should strip the hand before playing hearts.
2. Accordingly, you ruff a diamond at trick three and cross
    to dummy with a trump, East shedding a club. You then
    play your three top clubs discarding hearts, and ruff a club,
    West shedding a diamond on the fourth club.

    You are now down to two trumps and three hearts in
    each hand. You lead a heart toward dummy and West plays
    the ♡ K. What do you do?

WHATTA HAND!   (SOLUTION)

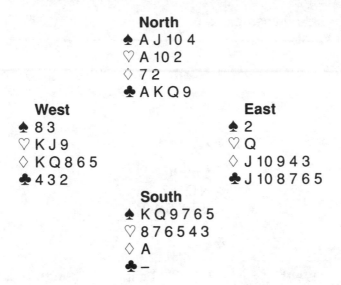

North
♠ A J 10 4
♡ A 10 2
◇ 7 2
♣ A K Q 9

West
♠ 8 3
♡ K J 9
◇ K Q 8 6 5
♣ 4 3 2

East
♠ 2
♡ Q
◇ J 10 9 4 3
♣ J 10 8 7 6 5

South
♠ K Q 9 7 6 5
♡ 8 7 6 5 4 3
◇ A
♣ —

Win the trick, reenter your hand with a trump and lead a second heart toward the ten. It's all a matter of counting.

West is known to have started with five black cards. If he had a singleton king of hearts (in which case it would be right to duck the trick) he would have started with seven diamonds headed by the KQ. Why didn't he bid? Because he didn't have seven diamonds to the KQ, that's why.

You happen to be playing against a West player who can also count. He knows you started with 6-6 in the majors, and he knows that if he plays the ♡ 9 you can insure your contract by playing the ♡ 10.

He knows that his partner needs the stiff ♡ Q to have any chance to defeat the contract. He knows that if you duck the ♡ K and he plays a second heart you are going to have to guess whether East started with the blank queen or QJ doubleton.

You can avoid this guess by winning the ♡ A and leading up to the ♡ 10.

KEY LESSON POINTERS

1. WHEN STRIPPING A HAND, IT IS NOT ALWAYS NECESSARY TO DRAW TRUMPS BEFORE BEGINNING THE STRIP. YOU MAY NEED THE TRUMPS FOR ENTRIES. HERE, FOR EXAMPLE, IT IS MORE CONVENIENT TO RUFF A DIAMOND BEFORE PLAYING THE SECOND SPADE.

2. WHEN DRAWING TRUMPS BE SURE TO LEAVE YOURSELF A FLEXIBLE TRUMP POSITION, i.e. FLUIDITY IN THE SUIT — THE ABILITY TO GET FROM ONE HAND TO THE OTHER. IN PLAIN ENGLISH, DO NOT BLOCK THE TRUMP SUIT.

3. MOST "GUESSES" CAN BE RESOLVED BY COUNTING. MOST OF THEM TURN OUT NOT TO BE GUESSES AFTER ALL.

(49) WHAT A DIFFERENCE A LEAD MAKES

Neither side vulnerable
Dealer North

North
♠ 9 4 2
♡ Q J 9
◇ K J
♣ A J 9 7 6

South
♠ J 10 8
♡ A 10 8
◇ A 3 2
♣ K Q 10 5

North	East	South	West
1 ♣	Pass	2 NT	Pass
3 NT	All Pass		

Opening Lead: ◇ 10

1. How do you play if the lead of the ten denies a higher honor?
2. How do you play if the lead of the ten does not deny a higher honor?

WHAT DIFFERENCE A LEAD MAKES (SOLUTION)

North
♠ 9 4 2
♡ Q J 9
◇ K J
♣ A J 9 7 6

West
♠ A Q 7
♡ K 6 2
◇ 10 9 8 6
♣ 4 3 2

East
♠ K 6 5 3
♡ 7 5 4 3
◇ Q 7 5 4
♣ 8

South
♠ J 10 8
♡ A 10 8
◇ A 3 2
♣ K Q 10 5

1.   If you "know" that East has the ◇ Q, you should play the ◇ K at trick one and run the ♡ Q.

Assuming it loses, West is going to have to be pretty shrewd to shift to a spade. (He doesn't know your clubs are running.)

Had you played the ◇ J at trick one, and had it been covered, you would have had to cross to a club to take the heart finesse. Once West "sees" what is going on in clubs, he will be able to count your tricks and find the spade shift.

2.   As there is a good chance that West has the ◇ Q, you should put in the ◇ J. After all, if it holds, you have nine tricks. If East plays the queen, the best you can do is win, cross to the ♣ A and run the ♡ Q. If it loses, hold your breath.

KEY LESSON POINTERS

1. IF THERE EVER WAS A HAND THAT INDICATES HOW IMPORTANT IT IS TO KNOW THE OPPONENTS' LEAD CONVENTIONS, THIS IS IT.
2. ON THIS PARTICULAR HAND IT IS MORE OF AN ADVANTAGE TO THE DECLAR-ER THAN THE DEFENDER TO KNOW THAT THE LEAD OF THE TEN DENIES A HIGHER HONOR.
3. NOTICE HOW MUCH MORE DECEPTIVELY DECLARER CAN PLAY THE HAND IF HE "KNOWS" TO WIN THE ◇ K AT TRICK ONE. HE DOES NOT HAVE TO EX-POSE HIS STRENGTH IN CLUBS.
4   AS DECLARER, WITH AN UNSTOPPED SUIT (SPADES) AND THE LIKELIHOOD OF LOSING THE LEAD, YOU DO NOT WANT YOUR OPPONENTS TO BE ABLE TO COUNT YOUR TRICKS IN THE OTHER SUITS. BY FINESSING HEARTS BEFORE TOUCHING CLUBS YOU ENCHANCE YOUR CHANCES OF A DIAMOND CONTINU-ATION.

(50) THANKS, PARTNER (1) (2) (3)

Neither side vulnerable
Dealer West

North
♠ A 7 3
♡ A K 10 3 2
◇ Q 5 4
♣ A Q

South
♠ 5 4
♡ Q J 8 7 6
◇ K 10 7 2
♣ 7 2

West	North	East	South
1 ♠	Dbl.	2 ♠	3 ♡
Pass	4 ♡	All Pass	

Opening Lead: ♠ K

1. Do you win this trick or do you duck?
   You duck the trick.
2. West continues with the ♣ Q. What is your plan?
   You should win the ♠ A, and ruff a spade, as East plays the ♠ J. You should continue with two rounds of trumps. East discards a club on the second round.
3. Now what?
   You play the ♣ A and the ♣ Q! Why?
   Because if West has the ♣ K he is endplayed and you can lose no more than one diamond trick; therefore you lose nothing even if the finesse is on. If East has the ♣ K he has to break diamonds.
4. East wins the ♣ K and shifts to a low diamond. Which diamond do you play? Why?

THANKS, PARTNER   (SOLUTION)

North
♠ A 7 3
♡ A K 10 3 2
◇ Q 5 4
♣ A Q

West
♠ K Q 10 9 8
♡ 9 4
◇ A J 9
♣ J 6 4

East
♠ J 6 2
♡ 5
◇ 8 6 3
♣ K 10 9 8 5 3

South
♠ 5 4
♡ Q J 8 7 6
◇ K 10 7 2
♣ 7 2

4.   The ◇ K. Although it isn't 100% clear that West has both the ace and jack of diamonds, it is extremely likely.

What kind of an opening bid does West have? He has a marriage in spades five times, no honors in hearts, and at most ♣ J for a total of 6 high card points. He is a big favorite to hold both diamond honors. If he does, your play of the ◇ K handcuffs him completely.

KEY LESSON POINTERS

1. AS A MATTER OF COURSE, IT IS USUALLY RIGHT TO DUCK AN OPENING LEAD HOLDING Axx FACING xx. IT IS BETTER TO ALLOW THE OPPONENTS TO WIN AN EARLY TRICK RATHER THAN A LATER ONE IN MOST CASES. THIS ASSUMES, OF COURSE, THAT YOU HAVE NO PARKING PLACE FOR YOUR LOSER.
2. SOMETIMES AN AQ SUIT CAN BE AN ILLUSION. IN THIS HAND IT IS. HERE IT DOESN'T MATTER IF YOU CAN PLAY THE ACE AND THEN THE QUEEN, AND WEST HAS THE KING. UPON WINNING THE TRICK, HE WILL HAVE TO BREAK DIAMONDS AND YOU WILL IMMEDIATELY GET YOUR TRICK BACK. THE REAL GAIN ACCRUES WHEN EAST HAS THE ♣ K. NOW HE HAS TO BREAK DIAMONDS AND THAT COULD BE A REAL GAINER FOR YOU.
3. SUITS THAT ARE DIVIDED TWO OPPOSITE TWO CAN FREQUENTLY BE USED AS THROW-IN SUITS — EVEN AQ OPPOSITE TWO SMALL. FINESSES ARE FOR CHILDREN.

APPENDIX (THEMES)

SECTION I (PLAY HANDS)

1. DECEPTION, READING THE LEAD
2. CARD COMBINATIONS
3. DECEPTION OF EQUAL HONOR MANAGEMENT. STRIP AND END PLAY.
4. ENTRY CONSERVATION, LOSER ON LOSER PLAY
5. PLANNING A TRUMP COUP.
6. CARD COMBINATIONS, PLACING THE OPPONENTS' HONORS FROM THE BIDDING
7. PARTIAL STRIP
8. CARD COMBINATIONS, EQUAL HONOR MANAGEMENT
9. CARD COMBINATIONS, INFERENCES
10. PLACING THE CARDS, PUTTING PRESSURE ON THE STRONG HAND BY FORCING DISCARDS.
11. AVOIDANCE, THROW IN PLAY, AVOIDING A FINESSE AT ALL COSTS
12. SEEING AN UNBLOCK — EARLY
13. CARD COMBINATIONS, UNBLOCKING
14. READING THE LEAD, AVOIDING A POSSIBLE DANGEROUS SHIFT
15. DECEPTION, LONG SUIT ESTABLISHMENT
16. PLACING THE CARDS FROM AN ORIGINAL PASS. REMOVING AN EXIT CARD PREMATURELY FROM AN OPPONENT'S HAND
17. RULE OF 11, DECEPTION
18. LOSER ON LOSER PLAY, SIMPLE SQUEEZE
19. THROW IN AND END PLAY, CARD COMBINATIONS
20. DECEPTION
21. PLACING THE CARDS FROM THE BIDDING, PLAYING TO MAKE, VISUALIZING WHAT THE DEFENSE CAN DO TO YOU (THROWING THE DUMMY ON LEAD) AND TAKING EARLY MEASURES TO AVOID THE STING.
22. PERCENTAGE PLAY
23. CARD COMBINATIONS, DECEPTION
24. OPERATING A TRUMP COUP, PLACING THE CARDS
25. CARD COMBINATIONS, LONG SUIT ESTABLISHMENT

SECTION II (DEFENSIVE HANDS)

SECTION III (DEFENSIVE HANDS)

26. THIRD HAND PLAY, CARD COMBINATIONS
27. FOILING A CROSSRUFF WITH A BRAVE DISCARD
28. CARD COMBINATIONS, INFERENCES, AVOIDING AN ENDPLAY
29. COUNTING THE HAND, CARD COMBINATIONS
30. COUNTING THE HAND, DISCARDING INSTEAD OF RUFFING TO FORCE DECLARER TO LOSE CONTROL, TRUMP MANAGEMENT DURING THE FORCING GAME
31. FINDING A FOURTH ROUND RUFF INGENIOUSLY, INFERENCES, VISUALIZING CARDS IN PARTNER'S HAND, LOCKING DECLARER IN DUMMY
32. READING PARTNER'S DISCARD, CARD COMBINATIONS
33. COUNTING DECLARER'S HAND — ASSUMING THE MOST LIKELY DISTRIBUTION, GIVING PARTNER A DELAYED RUFF
34. CARD COMBINATIONS, WHEN FACED WITH A CHOICE OF EVILS, KNOWING WHICH IS THE LESSER EVIL
35. KILLING A HAND ENTRY BY VISUALIZING A BLOCKED SUIT AND KNOCKING OUT THE ENTRY PREMATURELY
36. PLAYING FOR A SIMPLE, RATHER THAN A COMPLICATED SET, READING THE SPOTS
37. DECEPTION, CARD COMBINATIONS, LOCKING DECLARER IN DUMMY
38. AVOIDING AN ENDPLAY, READING DECLARER'S INTENTIONS AND FOILING THEM, TRUMP MANAGEMENT
39. GIVING PARTNER AN EARLY RUFF OF ONE OF YOUR GOOD TRICKS SO THAT HE CAN LEAD A SUIT YOU CAN'T
40. INFERENCES, CARD COMBINATIONS, AVOIDING A LATER ENDPLAY
41. COUNTING DECLARER'S TRICKS, FINDING THE WINNING DISCARD
42. COUNTING DECLARER'S HAND, TRUMP MANAGEMENT, LOCKING DECLARER IN DUMMY, TRUMP MANAGEMENT
43. UNBLOCKING TO AVOID AN ENDPLAY, COUNTING TRICKS
44. READING THE LEAD, KILLING THE DUMMY
45. WATCHING PARTNER'S COUNT SIGNALS, VISUALIZING AN ENDPLAY AND AVOIDING IT, COUNTING DECLARER'S HAND
46. CARD COMBINATIONS, SECOND HAND PLAY
47. READING THE LEAD, TRUMP PROMOTION
48. COUNTING DECLARER'S HAND, CARD COMBINATIONS
49. INFERENCES, COUNTING DECLARER'S TRICKS, NOT BEING AFRAID TO LEAD FROM AN AQ COMBINATION
50. COUNTING DECLARER'S HAND, CARD COMBINATIONS, SURROUNDING PLAYS

SECTION IV (PLAY HANDS)

26. PLACING THE CARDS
27. PLANNING A CROSSRUFF, COUNTING TRICKS
28. PARTIAL STRIP
29. COUNTING, CARD COMBINATIONS
30. OVERCOMING A BAD TRUMP DIVISION, PLACING THE CARDS WHERE YOU NEED THEM, VISUALIZING HARMFUL DISCARDS
31. PLAYING SAFE, CARD COMBINATIONS
32. DECEPTION WITH EQUAL HONORS, TRYING TO KEEP THE DANGEROUS HAND OFF LEAD
33. COUNTING, PLAYING THE PERCENTAGES
34. PLACING THE CARDS, CARD COMBINATIONS
35. COUNTING TRICKS, PLAYING TO MAKE, USING LIMITED HAND ENTRIES WISELY
36. MANDATORY DECEPTION
37. ENTRY CONSERVATION, CARD COMBINATIONS, HONOR MANAGEMENT
38. DEVELOPING AN ENTRY IN THE TRUMP SUIT, CATERING TO A BLOCKED SUIT, PLAYING AS SAFE AS POSSIBLE
39. USING THE BIDDING TO YOUR ADVANTAGE, INFERENCES, TRUMP MANAGEMENT, ENTRIES
40. STRIPPING THE HAND, ATTACKING THE RIGHT SUIT FIRST, LOSER ON LOSER PLAY
41. FORCING A DISCARD BEFORE COMMITTING
42. CONTROLLING THE PLAY WITH A TWO-SUITER, SCRAMBLING
43. COUNTING THE HAND, THROW IN AND ENDPLAY
44. UNBLOCKING TO CREATE A FINESSE POSITION, ENTRIES
45. VISUALIZING A BLOCKED SUIT, PLANNING A STRIP AND END PLAY, TRUMP MANAGEMENT, ENTRIES
46. PLANNING THE PLAY, ENTRIES, UNBLOCKING
47. PLAYING TO MAKE, RUFFING A WINNER, CARD COMBINATIONS
48. ENTRIES, CARD COMBINATIONS, STRIP AND END PLAY
49. READING THE LEAD, DECEPTION
50. PLACING THE HONORS, AVOIDANCE, STRIP AND END PLAY

Bridge
01-7 Kantar, A NEW APPROACH TO PLAY AND DEFENSE, $9.95
22-X Kantar, A NEW APPROACH TO PLAY AND DEFENSE, VOL 2, $9.95

Cookbooks
30-0 THE BEST OF BRIDGE: ROYAL TREATS FOR ENTERTAINING, $12.95

Health & Fitness
04-1 Orsini, EXERCISE AND NUTRITION THE ATHLETE'S WAY, $12.95
05-X Orsini, IMPROVING SPORTS PERFORMANCE, $10.95
08-4 Fashion Academy, AMERICAN TEEN: THIRTEEN STEPS TO BEAUTY,
          $16.95
09-2 Gerson *et al.,* MEDICINE AND YOUR MONEY: How to Buy Wellness in
          Today's Health Care Market, $16.95
18-1 AFAA, AEROBICS: THEORY & PRACTICE, $15.95
19-X AFAA, AEROBICS: A SELF-STUDY WORKBOOK, $9.95
20-3 Seaney, SEVENTEEN MINUTES TO COMPLETE RELAXATION, $12.95
23-8 AFAA, YOUR AEROBIC FITNESS ADVISOR, $12.95

Recreation/Scuba Diving
00-9 Frame, DIVER'S ALMANAC: GUIDE TO THE WEST COAST, $23.95
17-3 Guettermann, DIVERS ALMANAC: GUIDE TO THE BAHAMAS AND
          CARIBBEAN, $24.95

Business & Personal Finance
03-3 Adler, THE MAGIC SELL: A Seven Step Approach
          for Consumer Electronics, $16.95
21-1 Fenelli, THE FINANCIAL PROBLEM SOLVER, $10.95
25-4 Cathcart, SELLING — TWO WIN: How to Get and Keep Customers,
          $12.95

Psychology, Self-Improvement, Social Issues, Religion
02-5 Foster, THE QUEST FOR LOVE & MONEY, $9.95
10-6 Mead & Balch, CHILD ABUSE AND THE CHURCH: A NEW MISSION, $9.95

Auto Maintenance — Video
11-4 Mears, OIL CHANGE, FILTERS AND LUBE, $23.95
12-2 Mears, REPLACING SHOCKS AND STRUTS, $23.95
13-0 Mears, REPLACING EXHAUST SYSTEMS, $23.95
14-9 Mears, DETAILING, $23.95
15-7 Mears, TUNE-UP AND MAINTENANCE, $23.95
16-5 Mears, BODY & FENDER REPAIR, $23.95

ORDER FORM

HDL PUBLISHING COMPANY
702B Randolph Avenue
Costa Mesa, CA 92626

(714) 540-5775

_____ Please send me the following books:

QTY	AUTHOR	TITLE	PRICE
___	_____	_____	_____
___	_____	_____	_____
___	_____	_____	_____
___	_____	_____	_____
___	_____	_____	_____
___	_____	_____	_____

Total for books .... _____

California residents please add 6 1/2% sales tax   _____

Shipping & handling ($1.50 first book, $.50 each additional).. _____

ENCLOSE CHECK OR MONEY ORDER AND
HDL PAYS POSTAGE AND HANDLING.

TOTAL .... _____

_____ I enclose check or money order

_____ Please bill me, including shipping & handling charges

_____
Name

_____
Address

_____   _____   _____
City   State   Zip